LIKE A THIEF IN THE NIGHT

Preparing For the Second Coming of Christ

Jim Biscardi, Jr.

Copyright February 21, 2011
James Biscardi, Jr.

ISBN 978-0-9753786-5-6

Published by Mantle Ministries, PO Box 248, Lanoka Harbor, NJ 08734

All Rights Reserved

No part of this publication may be reproduced or transmitted in any form or by any means, electronic, or mechanical including photocopying, recording, or any information storage and retrieval system, without permission in writing from the publisher.

Cover artwork by Spiritlessons.com

Cover Design by Jim Biscardi, Jr.

TABLE OF CONTENTS

Introduction	5
How Close Is The Second Coming of the Lord?	7
How To Watch And Wait For Christ	13
Lock All The Windows And Doors	21
Take Inventory of All Your Household Goods	31
Change All The Locks	39
Turn On The Outside Lights	45
Get Your Weapons Of Protection Ready	51
Make Sure You Have An Escape Plan	61
The "Thief" Comes In The Twinkling Of An Eye	69
The "Thief" Becomes Our Judge – The Judgment Seat Of Christ	77
The "Thief" Becomes Our Bridegroom – A Marriage Made In Heaven	89
The "Thief" Becomes Our Commander-In-Chief – The Battle Of Armageddon	93
The "Thief" Becomes Our King – Ruling and Reigning With Christ	97
The "Thief" Becomes Our Eternal Residence Builder – The New Jerusalem	105
Topical Index	111

Many thanks to my Bible, Bagels and Blessings small group bible study partners who helped me know how to prepare if a thief were coming to break into our home.

Also, my very special thanks to my wife and partner in ministry, Patty, who encouraged me to pursue this project.

INTRODUCTION

Jesus told us to prepare for His coming like we would if a thief were coming to rob our home. This is an apt illustration when you consider that at His coming He will "steal" away all those who have trusted Him as their personal Lord and Savior. In $1/20^{th}$ of a second (i.e. in the blink of an eye), Christians all over the world will disappear, and, along with the dead in Christ who will be raised with immortal bodies, be caught up to meet the Lord in the air. And forever they will live, rule, and reign with Him.

I've been teaching God's Word for over 37 years. When I was preparing to teach our regular "Bible, Bagels, and Blessings" bible study, I believe the Lord dropped into my mind the idea of **literally** preparing for His coming like we would do if a thief were going to break into our homes. What would we do, and how could that relate to the Christian life? I asked the class what they would do to be ready for a thief. We came up with the following activities and relationships to how we live as Christians:

Watch and wait – Are we watching our behaviors? Are we waiting upon the Lord? There were ten "virgins" but the Lord only took five.

Lock all the doors and windows – Are we living a disciplined Christian life? Are we following the markers set out by the Lord on the race track of life?

Take inventory of all your household goods – What would Jesus find on a journey through the rooms of our heart? Would He want us to remove the clutter of life?

Change the locks – What are the buttons people can push in our lives that will arouse wrong emotions and behaviors? Are there keys to our heart that need to be changed?

Turn on the outside lights – How is our witness to a lost and dying world? Have we produced good works that light up the place we live so others can find Christ?

Get your weapons of protection ready – Has the Lord given us weapons of warfare and ways to win the spiritual battles we must endure here? Are we using them as prescribed by God?

Make sure you have an escape plan – What's the escape plan for non-Christians? Do born-again Christians need and have an escape plan?

Besides describing these behaviors in detail, *"Like a Thief in the Night"* explains how the "thief" becomes our Judge, Bridegroom, Commander-in-Chief, King, and the Builder of our forever home.

The dawn of the Lord's return is drawing ever closer. It is evident from the signs of His coming that our generation could very well be alive when He calls us home. We must as Jesus said, "Be ready."

"Till The Net Is Full" (John 21:8)

Jim Biscardi, Jr. Author

CHAPTER 1

HOW CLOSE IS THE SECOND COMING OF CHRIST?

As a young Christian in 1971, I thought the Lord's return was imminent. So I began to spend money "like a drunken sailor", thinking that there was no need to save or prepare for the future. Thank God, He quickly guided me to prepare for the future as if He wouldn't return for a long time, but to live my life like He was coming back tomorrow!

You might ask, "Doesn't every generation think the Second Coming is near?" I think that was probably done by God's design. The Lord wants us to be living representations of His sacrificial love in every generation. So He wants us to live our lives, look forward, and prepare to meet Him at any moment. Having said that, we know there is a generation that will, indeed, be alive when He returns. And it appears more and more certain that we may be that very generation. Here are some signs of Christ's return that couldn't have happened until NOW:

The Gospel will be preached in all the world before the physical return of Jesus Christ to the earth occurs at Armageddon. Exhaustive efforts are presently underway to accomplish this that could not have happened till our generation. Just think of what the internet and the social networks did to mobilize people in Tunisia and then in Egypt to eject their rulers.

That power is being used to get the Gospel out also. Matthew 24:14.

Humanity will be able to cross the globe rapidly and science will be advancing. Daniel 12:4. Knowledge has increased more in the last 50 years than in all the past years put together. Besides the advancement of science, the world itself has become a "global neighborhood" because of today's transportation systems.

The earth will be swimming in a sea of violence. As it was in the days of Noah (Luke 17:26), so it shall be at the end. How was the earth in Noah's time? Genesis 6:11 says, *"The earth also was corrupt before God, and the earth was filled with violence."* Crime in our streets is increasing year after year. Our schools have children killing children. Murders are more gruesome than ever before. Gang violence has spread like fire never being quenched by law enforcement.

There will be warfare all over the globe. Mark 13:8 says, *"For nation shall rise against nation, and kingdom against kingdom."* The terrorism threat is global. Not only is the USA threatened, but also Russia, India, Pakistan, Spain, England, Yemen, and many other countries.

Mankind will have the capability to destroy all life on the planet. Unique to our generation, this prophecy could not have been fulfilled prior to the invention of weapons of mass destruction such as the nuclear bomb. Matthew 24: 22 says, *"And except those days should be shortened, there should no flesh be saved: but for the elect's sake those days shall be shortened."*

Deadly diseases will be rampant, famines will be common, and earthquakes will be occurring globally. Matthew 24:7. Earthquakes are on the rise. Most earthquakes happen on the Pacific Rim. They experience 90% of the world's earthquakes. Japan alone has 1500 tremors a year. Our scientific equipment picks up about one million tremors around the world every year. The Geological Survey which has recorded quakes since 1900, now expects about eighteen 7.0 magnitude or larger quakes a year, and one 8.0 magnitude or larger quake. With each of them comes famine and disease.[1]

Some recent examples include:

May 2008 – 7.9 magnitude in China killing 69,000 people

January 2010 – Haitian quake killed 230,000 people

February 2010 – 8.8 magnitude Chilean quake - the 5th largest since 1900.

February 2010 – 7.0 magnitude in Japan

February 2011 – 6.3 magnitude in Christchurch, New Zealand

Christians and Jews will be hated for their faith in connection with Christ. Luke 21:17 says, *"And ye shall be hated of all men for my name's sake."* It seems like Israel can't do anything right. The U.N. is always condemning them. Israel builds a wall to defend itself or builds settlements for their people – or retaliates for a Palestinian bomb attack. They are always in the wrong. In the U.S., it seems that political correctness applies to other religions but not to Christians. The ACLU fights against any public prayer ending "in the name of Christ." There can't be prayer in school, or at sports events, or at town council meetings. You can wear a sweatshirt to school that is almost pornographic, but teachers cannot wear a cross!

There will be progress made toward a global government. The European Union, the revived Roman Empire, is alive today and moving steadily toward the fulfillment of this prophecy as seen in

---

[1] Earthquakes and Volcanoes in Prophecy, David C. Pack, March 2010

Daniel 7: 23. There are many groups that have been working to bring about world government in our generation (e.g. Club of Rome; Council on Foreign Relations; Trilateral Commission; Bilderberg Group; and the International Monetary Fund).

Global means of communication will exist. We know this because the book of Revelation teaches us that the entire world will see some events:

The return of Christ – *"...every eye shall see him..."* (Revelation 1:7)

The two witnesses of Revelation who will be killed for testifying about Christ – *"Their bodies will lie in the street of the great city...For three and a half days men from every people, tribe, language and nation will gaze on their bodies and refuse them burial"* (Revelation 11:9).

Today we see live news events streaming from any country via the internet. This is unique to our generation as only recently in mankind's history have these technologies been present.

In the last days, fallen angels will mingle with mankind. This one is very controversial, but there is a scriptural basis for this, as seen in Luke 17:26. *"And as it was in the days of Noah, so shall it be also in the days of the Son of man."* A careful examination of what was going on in Noah's day seems to suggest fallen angels were somehow mingling with mankind. Genesis 6:4. There is potentially more to the numerous UFO sightings and alien abduction stories in the news today than we have ever imagined!

Israel will exist as a nation in the latter days. Read Ezekiel 37:1-14 to see this prophecy, which was fulfilled in 1948.

Israel's birth as a nation will have happened in one day. Fulfilled on May 14, 1948 as seen in Isaiah 66:8

Israel will be surrounded on every side by enemies. Psalm 83:4 says, *"They have said, Come, and let us cut them off from being a nation; that the name of Israel may be no more in remembrance."* Besides the Palestinians and terrorists like Hamas and Hezbollah, Iran has made clear its intentions to wipe Israel off the map. The Tunisian people over threw their dictator ruler. Then it spread to Egypt, which borders Israel. Will other nations in the Middle East demand freedom from oppression – like Algeria, Jordan, and Saudi Arabia? Will radical anti-Israel religious groups take over these countries? As former US Secretary of State, 1989-1992, James Baker has said, "When the "freedom genie" is let out of the bottle, you don't know where it will spread."[2]

Technology will exist capable of tracking the world's population and finances. Revelation 13:16-17 says, *"And he causeth all, both small and great, rich and poor, free and bond, to receive a mark in their right hand, or in their foreheads: And that no man might buy or sell, save he that had the mark, or the name of the beast, or the number of his name."*

Several years ago, I discovered that over 200 U.S. hospitals were placing computer chips in humans. These chips can be used for GPS tracking purposes. Parents can do that for children so they cannot be kidnapped without detection. Recently, in the US, 30 million dollars was appropriated to automate medical records. These can be put on chips and implanted in humans.

The Universal Product Code is placed on almost everything we buy and sell today. This UPC code is formatted with a start bar, then the manufacturer, then a middle bar, then the product, then an end bar. The start, middle, and end bars are the number 6, making it 666.

---

[2] Fox News, Special Report with Bret Baier, February 2, 2011

The capability will exist for an army of 200 million soldiers to be formed. In Revelation 9:16, John sees a specific number of soldiers (i.e. "horsemen") preparing for or entering into war. *"And the number of the army of the horsemen were two hundred thousand thousand: and I heard the number of them."* As of 2006, China had an estimated (by CIA) 281,240,272 men fit for military service.

CHAPTER 2

HOW TO WATCH AND WAIT FOR CHRIST

HOW SHOULD WE PREPARE FOR CHRIST'S RETURN?

Our Lord Jesus Christ told us how to get ready for His second coming. He wants us to prepare as if we knew that a thief was coming to break into our home to steal, kill, and destroy. Speaking about His return, He said, *"Do not be afraid, little flock, for your Father has been pleased to give you the kingdom. Sell your possessions and give to the poor. Provide purses for yourselves that will not wear out, a treasure in heaven that will not be exhausted, where no thief comes near and no moth destroys. For where your treasure is, there will your heart be also."*

"Let your waist be girded and your lamps burning [that is, be prepared]; and you yourselves be like men who wait for their master, when he will return from the wedding, that when he comes and knocks they may open to him immediately. Blessed are those servants whom the master, when he comes, will find watching. . . . And if he should come in the second watch, or come in the third watch, and find them so, blessed are those servants. But know this, **that if the master of the house had known what hour the thief would come, he would have watched and not allowed his house to be broken into. Therefore you also be ready, for the Son of Man is coming at an hour you do not expect"** (Luke 12:32–40).

Remember what Jesus said about the thief in John 10: 9, *"I am the gate; whoever enters through me will be saved. The thief comes only to steal and kill and destroy..."*

WATCH AND WAIT FOR THE "THIEF"

One of the most important scriptures in God's Word is Luke 12: 39-40 *"...if the master of the house had known what hour the thief would come, he would have watched and not allowed his house to be broken into. Therefore you also be ready for the Son of Man is coming at an hour you do not expect."*

We are the master of our house (i.e. our body, soul, and spirit). We are the ones who must be "watching" to prevent the thief from breaking in. So what do we need to do to be ready when Christ returns? The answer is the same as asking, "What would we do if we knew a thief was coming to break into our house?"

One of the things we would do is to keep watching & waiting. Are we watching the way we are running the Christian race? Are we obeying Hebrews 12:1-2 to throw off everything that hinders and the sin that so easily entangles us, and to run with perseverance the race marked out for us? Are we fixing our eyes on Jesus, the author and finisher of our faith?

Though it may vary slightly from verse to verse, numerous instructions are given to "*watch*, because the Day of the Lord [i.e. or else Christ Himself] will come *as a thief in the night*"

WHAT ARE WE WATCHING FOR?

A familiar "watching" verse is Luke 21:36: *"Watch therefore, and pray always that you may be counted worthy to escape all these things that will come to pass, and to stand before the Son of Man."* It is frequently interpreted to mean that we should be closely watching current events so we know how close we are to Christ's return.

We can tell from the context, however, that Jesus has something else in mind. Verse 36 begins, *"Watch therefore,"* indicating that it refers to previous material. *"But take heed to yourselves, lest your hearts be weighed down with carousing, drunkenness, and cares of this life, and that Day come on you unexpectedly. For it will come as a snare on all those who dwell upon the face of the whole earth"* (Luke 21:34-35).

Clearly, the warning Jesus was giving us was more than just watching world events to know when He will return. Instead, His instruction is to watch <u>ourselves</u>, which is what "*take heed to yourselves*" suggests. He is talking about being alert to our own spiritual state, as well as being cautious and spiritually awake as we go through life. The danger is that, if we do not "watch" ourselves [i.e. regularly take stock of our condition and responsibilities] selfishness and material concerns will distract us, and we will find ourselves spiritually unprepared when Christ returns.[3]

So when Jesus says, *"Watch therefore, and pray always..."* (Luke 21:36), He's saying that besides praying we must "take heed" (i.e. constantly pay attention to ourselves), examining our walk and how we are seeking and emulating Him. The word translated "watch," implies being untouched by any influence that may cloud the mind. The person who "watches" is guarding against being sleepy or confused. Combined with "pray always," it means being alert for spiritual dangers and entrapments.

In Luke 12: 37-38, Jesus pronounces a blessing on those whom the Master finds watching *when* He returns. *"Blessed are those servants, whom the lord when he cometh shall find watching..."* It

---

[3] As A Thief In The Night, David C. Grabbe, Forerunner, "Prophecy Watch", July-August 2008

is not that they have their eyes peering into the night sky, watching *for* His return. Instead, those who are vigilant and careful in their responsibilities will be blessed. They are watching over the Master's house (i.e. we are the temple of the Holy Spirit) ensuring that all is in order, even if it means sleepless nights. *"Be ready"* in Luke 12: 40 is a simple summation of the "watching" He desires.

OTHER SCRIPTURES ABOUT WATCHING

In Luke 12: 42-47, the instruction to watch continues. However, this time Jesus focuses specifically on the responsibility of the steward—the one given authority over the household while the Master is away, *"And the Lord said, 'Who then is that faithful and wise steward, whom his master will make ruler over his household, to give them their portion of food in due season? Blessed is that servant whom his master will find so doing when he comes. Truly, I say to you that he will make him ruler over all that he has. But if that servant says in his heart, 'My master is delaying his coming,' and begins to beat the male and female servants, and to eat and drink and be drunk, the master of that servant will come on a day when he is not looking for him, and at an hour when he is not aware, and will cut him in two and appoint him his portion with the unbelievers. And that servant who knew his master's will, and did not prepare himself or do according to his will, shall be beaten with many stripes.'"*

His emphasis is on preparation and faithful continuance of duty. He tasks the steward—a type of leadership ministry—with giving the household " *their portion of food in due season.*" In a similar way, Paul gives the responsibilities of church leaders. *"And He Himself gave some to be apostles, some prophets, some evangelists, and some pastors and teachers, for the equipping of the saints for the work of ministry [service], for the edifying of the body of Christ. . ."* (Ephesians 4:11-13). Like the steward in Christ's parable, church leaders are responsible for feeding God's household and encouraging them to watch themselves.

If the leadership of a church, like the steward, doesn't properly watch, the human tendency is to let down—and even abuse others. The steward in Luke 12:45 is focused on the signs of the Master's return—or lack of signs —rather than on his own attention to his duties. As a result, he falls into excesses of eating and drinking, and hurting members of the household, rather than providing food for them. So those who have leadership responsibilities in the church have an added weight to *"take heed to themselves"* lest they neglect or even damage those for whom they are supposed to be providing spiritual food.[4]

Another example of watching is in Mark 13:32-37, *"But of that day and hour no one knows, not even the angels in heaven, nor the Son, but only the Father. Take heed, watch and pray; for you do not know when the time is. It is like a man going to a far country, who left his house and gave authority to his servants, and to each his work, and commanded the doorkeeper to watch. Watch therefore, for you do not know when the master of the house is coming—in the evening, at midnight, at the crowing of the rooster, or in the morning—lest, coming suddenly, he find you sleeping. And what I say to you, I say to all: Watch!"*

In this parable, it is even more apparent that the Master intends for the servants to be diligent, alert, taking heed to themselves in their work and authority rather than in His return. Twice, He says that no one knows the timing of His return—not even Him! He tells us that we do not know the "day and hour."

The Parable of the Wise and Foolish Virgins in Matthew 25:1-13 uses a different metaphor, but the warning is the same. A shout awakens them all at midnight. There's no time for preparation. The Bridegroom has arrived and they are commanded to meet Him. Five of them are ready. They have made the necessary preparations. But for the other five, there's no time to get things

---

[4] Ibid

into shape. There's no more time to grow, overcome, develop a relationship with the Father and the Son, and take on their character. There's no more time to be *"filled with the fruits of righteousness…to the glory and praise of God"* (Philippians 1:11).

The Bridegroom tells those who had not made advance spiritual preparations, *"I do not know you."* They lose out on the opportunity that God had given to them because they would not watch themselves.

In I Thessalonians, Paul also addresses the Day of the Lord coming as a thief in the night. *"But concerning the times and the seasons, brethren, you have no need that I should write to you. For you yourselves know perfectly that the day of the Lord so comes as a thief in the night. . . . But you, brethren, are not in darkness, so that this Day should overtake you as a thief. You are all sons of light and sons of the day. We are not of the night nor of darkness. Therefore let us not sleep, as others do, but let us watch and be sober. For those who sleep, sleep at night, and those who get drunk are drunk at night. But let us who are of the day be sober, putting on the breastplate of faith and love, and as a helmet the hope of salvation. For God did not appoint us to wrath, but to obtain salvation through our Lord Jesus Christ"* I Thessalonians 5:1-2, 4-9.

Like us, the return of Christ was much on the minds of first-century Christians, yet Paul tells them that he felt no need to write concerning its timing. Why? Because they should have known that the Day of the Lord will come like a thief in the night. There was no point in Paul trying to outline it all, as it will happen at a time that nobody can anticipate.

HOW SHOULD WE WAIT?

Waiting for the "thief" should be done patiently, proactively, serving Christ by serving others:

We need to wait patiently. *"Therefore, since we are surrounded by such a great cloud of witnesses, let us throw off everything that hinders and the sin that so easily entangles, and let us run with perseverance [patience] the race marked out for us. Let us fix our eyes on Jesus..."* (Hebrews 12:1).

"Rest in the Lord, and wait patiently for him: fret not thyself because of him who prospereth in his way, because of the man who bringeth wicked devices to pass...For evil doers shall be cut off: but those who wait on the Lord, they shall inherit the earth." (Psalm 37:7-11).

We need to wait proactively. *"Do not merely listen to the word, and so deceive yourselves. Do what it says. Anyone who listens to the word but does not do what it says is like a man who looks at his face in the mirror and, after looking at himself, goes away and immediately forgets what he looks like. But the man who looks intently into the perfect law that gives freedom, and continues to do this, not forgetting what he has heard but doing it – he will be blessed in what he does"* (James 1:22-24).

Also, remember the parable of the talents, where the master of the household goes on a long journey and gives his servants money according to their abilities. To one he gives five talents [of money], to another two, and to another one talent. The first two servants are proactive in investing and multiplying the master's money. The third went and buried his talent. When the master returned, he rewarded the first two servants, and said, *"Well done, thou good and faithful servant: thou hast been faithful over a few things, I will make thee ruler over many things: enter thou into the joy of thy lord"* (Matthew 25:21). But he reprimanded the unfaithful and lazy servant and said, *"Cast ye the unprofitable servant into outer darkness: there shall be weeping and gnashing of teeth"* (25:30).

While we wait, we need to be serving Christ by serving others. As the apostles were walking with the Lord, they began to argue about which one of them was the greatest. A little bit later, Jesus sat with them to celebrate the Passover meal, and to show them what it meant to be great in His kingdom, He took a towel wrapped it around Himself and began washing the disciples' feet. When He finished washing their feet, He put on His clothes and returned to His place.

Then He said to the disciples: *"Do you understand what I have done for you? You call me 'Teacher' and 'Lord,' and rightly so, for that is what I am. Now that I, your Lord and Teacher, have washed your feet, you also should wash one another's feet. I have set you an example that you should do as I have done for you...Once you know these things, you will be blessed if you do them"* (John 13: 1-17).

At another time, when Jesus was teaching His disciples not to be like the Pharisees and scribes, He said plainly, *"But he that is greatest among you shall be your servant. And whosoever exalts himself shall be abased: and he that shall humble himself shall be exalted"* (Matthew 23:11-12).

Remember Isaiah's advice about waiting upon the Lord: *"But they that wait upon the Lord shall renew their strength; they shall mount up with wings as eagles; they shall run, and not be weary; and they shall walk and not faint."* (Isaiah 40:31). Mounting up with *"wings as eagles"* sounds a lot like the Rapture! 1Thessalonians 4: 13-17.

CHAPTER 3

LOCK ALL THE WINDOWS AND DOORS

IS OUR LIFE A DISCIPLINED CHRISTIAN LIFE?

Just like we are disciplined to secure our homes by locking all the doors and windows (especially when we're not sure when a thief might break in), we also need to be disciplined in our spiritual life. Remember, our body is the temple of the Holy Spirit. We are a spiritual house, and we need to secure it by abiding in Christ. John 15:5

The disciplined Christian life is like riding a bicycle. The rim of

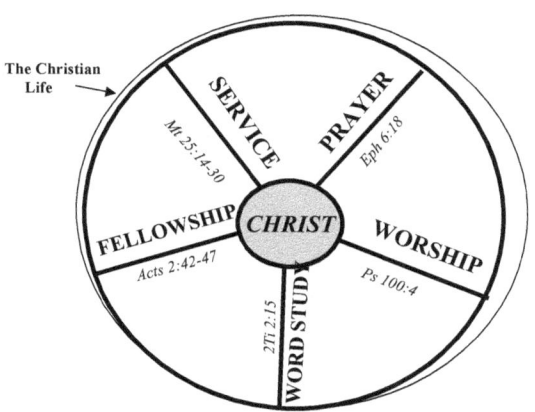

the wheel is the Christian life. The hub is Christ. We connect the Christian life to the hub [Christ] by spokes. These spokes cause us to "abide in Christ", to stay connected to Him. The spokes represent race course markers (like street signs for the New York marathon) we use to stay on course. They also represent the spiritual vitamins God has given to us to help us run the race of life with His strength. We should be regularly partaking of these spiritual vitamins as prescribed in God's Word, keeping them in balance as directed by the Great Physician:

- Vitamin A (Ask) **Prayer** – Ephesians 6:18
- Vitamin B (Bible) **Study the Word** – 2Timothy 2:15
- Vitamin C (Comfort Others) in their **Trials & Suffering** with the comfort God gave us in our own trials – 2Corinthians 1:4. Trials are not in our control. We trust God to provide whatever He deems appropriate.
- Vitamin D (Do) **Service** – Matthew 25:14-30, Romans 12, and 1Corinthians 12
- Vitamin E (Exalt) **Worship** – Psalm 100:4
- Vitamin K (Koinonia is a Greek word for fellowship) **Fellowship** – Acts 2:42-47.

We need to keep them in balance because if one or two spokes are longer than the others, it creates a bumpy ride for us. And if the spokes are too small, we have to pump very hard to cover just a small distance. We also need to have periods of rest and renewal. Mark 6:31.

These course markers and vitamins are what God uses to transform our lives into Christ's image by renewing our minds. Romans 12: 1-2 says, *"Therefore, I urge you, brothers, in view of God's mercy, to offer yourselves as living sacrifices, holy and pleasing to God – which is your spiritual worship. Do not conform any longer to the pattern of this world, but be transformed by the renewing of your mind. Then you will be able to test and approve what God's will is – his good, pleasing, and perfect will."*

The Transformation

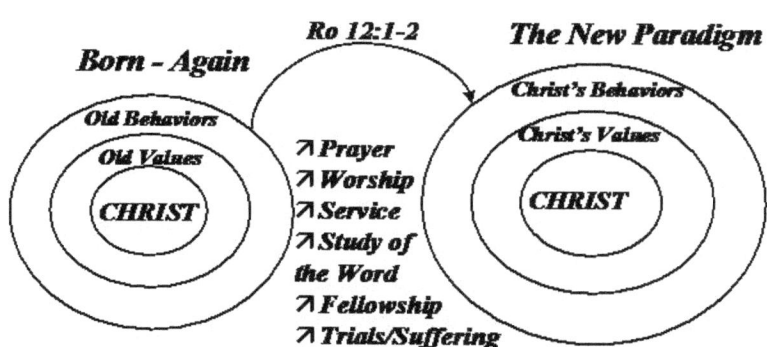

WHAT'S WORSHIP ALL ABOUT?

Worship to tell Him how much we love Him and how much we appreciate His work in our lives – to realize and enjoy being in His presence – to remind ourselves who He is and who we are in Christ. Worshipping the Lord reminds us that we fall way short of His greatness, and minimizes the differences we sometimes imagine between ourselves and other believers. So worship promotes unity in the Body of Christ. John 17:21.

Worship Him as the Lord and the One we serve. Enjoy His great love and acceptance of us as He shapes us into what He wants us to be. Remember, God loves us as we are, but He doesn't want us to stay that way. He wants to shape us into the image of His Son. Psalm 95: 1-6 gives us guidelines in worshipping our great God:

"O come, let us sing unto the Lord: let us make a joyful noise to the rock of our salvation. Let us come before his presence with thanksgiving, and make a joyful noise unto him with psalms. For

the Lord is a great God, and a great King above all gods. In his hands are the deep places of the earth: the strength of the hills is his also. The sea is his, and he made it: and his hands formed the dry land. O come, let us worship and bow down: let us kneel before the Lord our maker."

As we worship Him as our Lord, let's remember to be liberal in our giving to His work – our time, money, talents, and strength. *"But this I say, He which soweth sparingly shall reap also sparingly; and he which soweth bountifully shall also reap bountifully. Every man according as he purposeth in his heart, so let him give; not grudgingly, or of necessity: for God loveth a cheerful giver"* (2Corinthians 9:6-7).

Dave Brandon has said, "One way to worship God is to meditate on His many attributes. Exalt God for He is faithful, eternal, all knowing, just, unchangeable, gracious, holy, merciful, long suffering, impartial and infinite. Our God is perfect. Exalt Him by realizing that He is all-powerful, almighty, personal, righteous, unsearchable, wise, triune, accessible, self-existent, glorious, and compassionate.

"Another way to worship God is to contemplate His names. Exalt God, for He is Creator. He is Love. He is Redeemer. He is Shepherd. He is Savior, Lord, and Father. He is Judge. He is Comforter. He is Teacher. He is I AM. Our God is the Mighty One."[5]

WHAT'S FELLOWSHIP ALL ABOUT?

---

[5] Dave Brandon, Our Daily Bread, February 13, 2011

Lock All The Windows And Doors

We fellowship in Christ when we lovingly submit to each other (Ephesians 5:21), are accountable to one another, and share our lives with one another – our testimony, our victories and struggles, our appointments and disappointments - our relationship with Jesus Christ. We fellowship when we share how our Lord is both our "Giver" and "Taker" as we surrender our life to Him. We fellowship when we receive Christ from one another by obeying His "one another" instructions.

There are thirty "one another" scriptures in the New Testament. Let me highlight the following ones:

"Restore one another in the spirit of meekness" (Galatians 6:1). We need to learn how to minister to one another with "meekness" (i.e. to operate in God's strength, not our own, and to be sensitive to His slightest nudging). And, as people who need the help of our

remember...

*We don't appreciate **fellowship** until our natural man is dealt with through the disciplinary work of the Holy Spirit. When Jacob reached Hebron (Gen 35:27), he was ready for fellowship.*

When we reach Hebron, we are ready to receive Christ from others. That's what fellowship is all about...

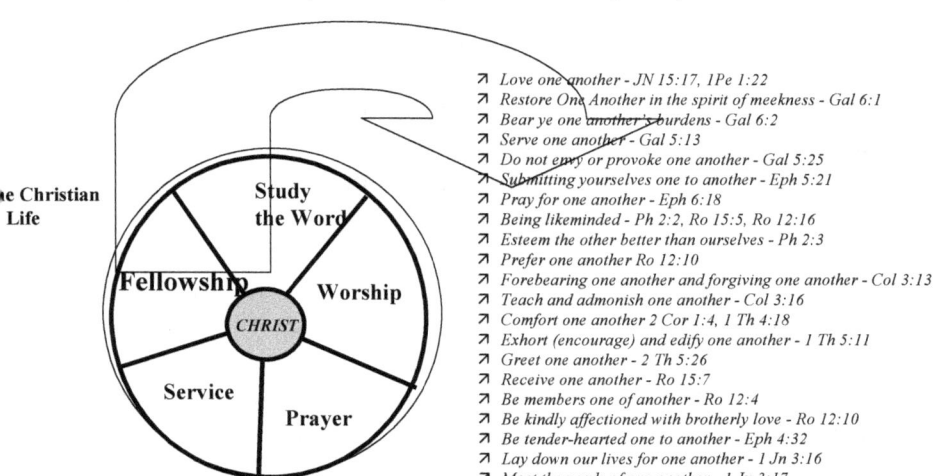

The Christian Life

- Study the Word
- Fellowship
- Worship
- CHRIST
- Service
- Prayer

↗ Love one another - JN 15:17, 1Pe 1:22
↗ Restore One Another in the spirit of meekness - Gal 6:1
↗ Bear ye one another's burdens - Gal 6:2
↗ Serve one another - Gal 5:13
↗ Do not envy or provoke one another - Gal 5:25
↗ Submitting yourselves one to another - Eph 5:21
↗ Pray for one another - Eph 6:18
↗ Being likeminded - Ph 2:2, Ro 15:5, Ro 12:16
↗ Esteem the other better than ourselves - Ph 2:3
↗ Prefer one another Ro 12:10
↗ Forebearing one another and forgiving one another - Col 3:13
↗ Teach and admonish one another - Col 3:16
↗ Comfort one another 2 Cor 1:4, 1 Th 4:18
↗ Exhort (encourage) and edify one another - 1 Th 5:11
↗ Greet one another - 2 Th 5:26
↗ Receive one another - Ro 15:7
↗ Be members one of another - Ro 12:4
↗ Be kindly affectioned with brotherly love - Ro 12:10
↗ Be tender-hearted one to another - Eph 4:32
↗ Lay down our lives for one another - 1 Jn 3:16
↗ Meet the needs of one another - 1 Jn 3:17

brethren, to learn how to receive correction as a blessing and not become disturbed by it.

"Do not envy or provoke one another" (Galatians 5:25). Sadly, competition and envy, so prevalent in the world, has entered the Body of Christ. We need to learn how to encourage one another in each of our ministries, and to help one another perfect our ministries to build up the church in the love and maturity of the Lord. Ephesians 4: 13 – 16.

"Esteem one another better than ourselves" (Philippians 2:3). This seems to be a shorthand way of describing how our love should be for one another. 1 Corinthians 13: 4-12. We need to lose our lives for Christ in order to gain real life. Jesus said it this way, *"A new commandment I give unto you that you love one another as I have loved you."* John 13: 34. Jesus gave His life for ours – now we need to give our lives for one another!

"Be members one of another" (Romans 12:4). We are so intimately connected and dependent upon one another that we can't function well without each other's support.

WHAT'S SERVICE ALL ABOUT?

Surrender for service to allow Him to use us for His glory and for honoring His name – to let Him bless us as a vessel He works through as fathers and husbands, mothers and wives, church leaders, workplace leaders, and believers fulfilling the Great Commission – to develop a heart in us for serving others (Luke 12:35) – to develop hearts in others we disciple for serving like He's developed in us.

Jesus told His disciples, *"Launch out into the deep, and let down your nets for a draught."* (Luke 5:4). Though they had fished all night and caught nothing, they obeyed the Master. They caught so many fish that their net was breaking and they had to call "their partners" to help them. As they did, let us be obedient to the Lord and overcome our fear to get into deep waters with Him, where the "fishing for souls" and making disciples is good. It's in deep water where we must depend upon His strength and not our own. Let's surrender for service as He calls us, overcome our fears, and trust Him to do the work through us by His Holy Spirit. **Till the net is full."** John 21:8.

HOW SHOULD WE PRAY?

Jesus gave us a pattern we should use when we pray. Matthew 6: 9-15. He told us first that we should not pray in order to get recognized by man. But He told us to enter our prayer closets where God alone hears and answers our prayers. He also cautioned us not to be repetitious, because our Father knows our requests before we ask. Then He told us to pray like this:

"Our Father" – God wants us to approach Him as "daddy". He desires intimacy with us.

"Which art in Heaven" - Fear and revere Him. He is all-powerful and can deal with all our problems.

"Hallowed be Thy name" – Approach God with awe and wonder. Save the word "awesome" for God. Live a life that honors Him. Isaiah 6:1

"Thy kingdom come" – Bloom where you are planted. Find your gifts and use them to build up the Body. God's kingdom is the rule of God in the hearts of His people by Jesus Christ.

"Thy will be done on earth as it is in heaven" – Surrender daily (Romans 12:1). Pray John 4:34 where Jesus said, *"My food is to do the will of him who sent me and to finish his work."* He is the potter, we are the clay. Keep your clay moist (pliable) through daily prayer. We need to keep a *"new wineskin"* heart that is flexible so the Lord can give us new truth! Luke 5: 37-38.

"Give us this day our daily bread" – Trust that God will supply all our needs. Philippians 4:19. My favorite song and lyrics are, "His eye is on the sparrow, and I know He watches me."

"Forgive our debts as we forgive our debtors" – Don't carry a burden of unforgiveness. Forgive others. Remember revealing the feeling is the beginning of healing. In our weakness God will send His strength and peace. Behave as if you have forgiven and the feeling will follow.

"Lead us not into temptation" – We are tempted every day. It deepens our walk and strengthens our faith. But be careful of spiritual blindness. Ask Him to open our spiritual eyes to our own blind spots, and to help us accept correction from honest friends and family. Even Jesus asked His disciples, *"Who do men say that I, the Son of Man, am"* (Luke 9:18)?

"Deliver us from evil" – Jesus is more powerful than Satan. He who is in us is greater than he that is in the world.

"For Thine is the kingdom and the power, and the glory forever" – This is our Father's world. Everything we have is His. He is the Ruler and Blessed Controller of all things.

WHY SHOULD WE STUDY GOD'S WORD?

The Word of God was written over a period of 1600 years by 40 different authors who wrote 66 books. Yet from Genesis to Revelation, this Book tells a consistent, unified story. The human writers were not afraid to acknowledge that what they wrote and spoke was given to them by God. Exodus 34:27, Acts 3: 18, 21, and Hebrews 1:1.

God's Word is a lamp unto our feet and a light unto our path. To me that means that His Word can help us moment by moment (the lamp) and also to do long-term planning (the light). Here are other reasons for disciplining our lives to study the Word of God:

Because God wrote it. 2Timothy 3:16
To ensure salvation. 2Timothy 3:15
To obtain hope. Romans 15:4
To avoid deception. Proverbs 28:26; Ephesians 5:6
To obtain faith. Romans 10:17
To obtain answers to prayer. John 15:7
To please God. Hebrews 11:6
To show ourselves approved unto God. 2 Timothy 2:15
To cleanse our souls through obedience. John 15:3; 1Peter 1:22
To become wise. Psalm 19:7
To learn righteousness. Isaiah 26:9; 2Timothy 3:16
To become sanctified. John 17:7; Acts 20:32
Because the Word will judge us on the Last Day. John 12:48
To avoid sin. Psalm 119:11
To save others. 1Timothy 4:15-16
To obtain the knowledge of God. Proverbs 2:1-6; Matthew 11:9
To avoid destruction. Hosea 4:6; Proverbs 13:13
To love God. John 14:15, 21-24
To understand God's will for our lives. Romans 12:2
To be able to do God's will. James 1:22
To avoid being ashamed when Jesus returns. Psalm 119:4-6
To grow in grace. 2Peter 1:2; Colossians 4:6
To confess Jesus. Luke 12: 8-9.
To obtain healing. Proverbs 4: 20-23
Because it will lead us and light our path. Psalm 119:105
To be transformed by the renewing of our mind, and become like Jesus. Romans 12: 1-2
To be partaker of the New Covenant. Hebrews 8:10-12

CHAPTER 4

TAKE INVENTORY OF ALL YOUR HOUSEHOLD GOODS

If a thief were coming to your house, you might want to inventory and take photographs of all your household goods for insurance purposes. Some folks do that as a regular habit when they get some new, pricy furniture, jewelry, computers and other technology toys that will be kept in their homes.

GETTING RID OF THE CLUTTER OF LIFE

During 1974-77, I lived in Stuttgart, Germany, working as a civilian for the Army at Patch Barracks. The Germans had a tradition that we Americans living there appreciated very much because we could fill up our apartments with household goods at no cost.

If the Germans had something they wanted to throw away, but didn't think that it belonged on the "*Trödelmarkt*" (fleamarket), they had the opportunity at certain announced times to place their stuff outside when *Sonstige-* or *Sperrmüll* (miscellaneous items) would be gathered by the garbage men. This could include a sofa, broken hi-fi, chairs, building materials, etc.

The funny thing was that not much of this stuff ended up on the garbage dump since many second hand dealers or "collectors" or apartment dwellers like me drove around the neighborhood to inspect the thrown out stuff. The majority of it got loaded into private vans long before the municipal vans came around! It became a matter of pride in neighborhoods to see which neighbor would throw out the best household "clutter!"

We Christians need to examine ourselves to see how much of "the world" has cluttered our hearts, and then get rid of it. We need to let Jesus take us on a journey through our own hearts, and throw away the things He doesn't want there. And also, let Him fill our hearts with the things that produce light in us and give Him glory.

IS OUR SPIRITUAL HOUSE IN ORDER?

What's in your heart's study room, living room, dining room, recreation room, bed room, and hall closet? Is He a guest there or is He Lord of the house? We need to get rid of the clutter of life!

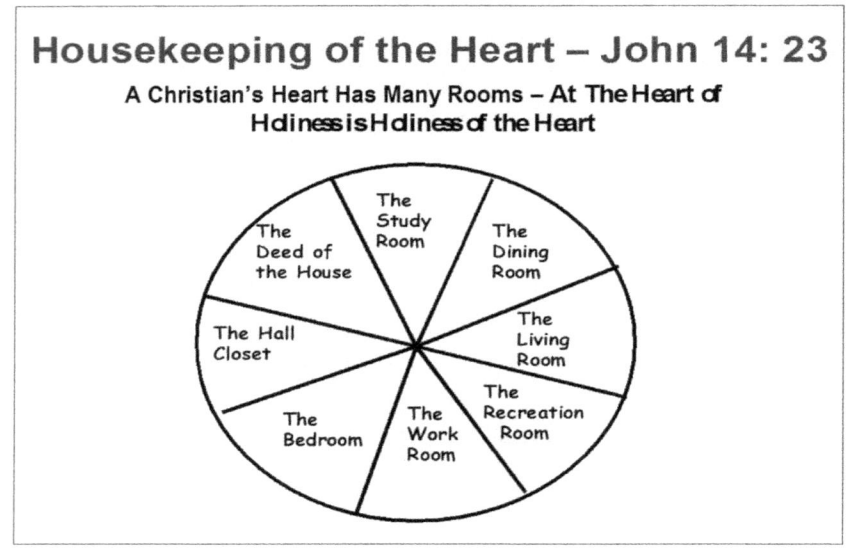

Before returning to the Father, Jesus said, *"Do not let your hearts be troubled. Trust in God; trust also in me. There are many rooms in my Father's house; otherwise, I would have told you. I am going to prepare a place for you. And if I go and prepare a place for you, I will come back and take you to be with me that you also may be where I am"* (John 14:1-3).

A short time later, He said, *"If anyone loves me, he will obey my teaching. My Father will love him, and we will come to him and make our home with him."* (John 14:23)

The word "place" in vs. 2-3 is the same word "home" in vs. 23. So as Jesus is preparing a home for us in heaven, we are to prepare a home for Him in our hearts.

Let's examine the rooms in our heart with Jesus[6]:

The Study Room - What would Jesus see in your mind? What are the magazines and books we read, or the videos and TV programs we watch? He would want His picture in the center of that room and the books of the scriptures on all the book shelves. *"Thou wilt keep him in perfect peace, whose mind is stayed on thee: because he trusteth in thee"* (Isaiah 26:3). *"Study to show thyself approved unto God, a workman that needeth not be ashamed, rightly dividing the word of truth"* (2Timothy 2:15).

The Dining Room - What would you serve Jesus? What are your appetites and desires? Is it your education, wealth, investments, awards, etc.? If so, Jesus would not eat much and would say, *"My food is to do the will of him who sent me and to finish his work"* (John 4:34).

The Living Room - This is the room where Jesus waits to meet with us every day. Do you read the Word and pray to Him daily?

---

[6] My Heart, Christ's Home, Robert Boyd Munger, 1986

He would tell us that that time is not just for us but also for Him. He paid a great price for us - and wants to meet and fellowship with us often. He's faithful to wait in the living room of our hearts for us – even when we miss our appointments with Him.

The Recreation Room - This is our place of fun and fellowship. Would the Lord find us taking Him with us when we go out with friends - or would we have to tell the Lord to wait home because He would feel uncomfortable? He would remind us that we were going to let Him be our Friend and go with us everywhere.

The Work Room - The Lord would look to see what we've done for Him lately. We might say that we felt awkward and clumsy in spiritual things. He would agree and tell us to put ourselves in the control of the Holy Spirit and let Him lead us in doing God's work. Some men asked Jesus, *"What shall we do, that we might work the works of God? Jesus answered and said to them, "This is the work of God, that you believe on him whom he hath sent"* (John 6:28-29).

The Bedroom - Here the Lord would remind us that He doesn't restrict sex to a marriage relationship because sex is bad but because it is good under the right conditions. When not in marriage, sex can be harmful and destructive.

The Hall Closet - As we are showing Jesus around our heart, He may pass the hall closet and mention that there's a horrible odor coming from there - maybe some stuff left over from our lives before we asked Him to come in. He'd want us to clean it. We would probably have to tell Him that we didn't have the strength - these things are too hard for us to "set aside". But we'd finally ask Him to clean it for us. Jesus would say that He'd been waiting for us to ask. Then, very soon thereafter the closet would be clean.

Then, one day, we would ask the Lord to clean **our whole house** like He did the hall closet. He would say, *"That's why I'm here.*

You can't live the Christian life alone." But what would the Lord say next to you and me. He might have to say, *"But I don't have the authority to clean your house because you've only made Me a guest here. First, you'll need to sign over the deed of your house to Me and make Me the owner."*

Sometimes we need to rededicate our lives to Jesus as <u>LORD</u>.

Remember that authentic Christianity means coming under the loving Lordship of Jesus Christ and being joined to a community of believers who are also on the journey of being shaped into Christ's image. The Greek word for "Lord" is "Kurios." It means one in absolute authority or supreme controller. It implies unbending allegiance to a supreme authority. It means an end to life on our own terms. So Jesus must be Lord of all or not Lord at all!

Jesus said, *"If anyone would come after me, he must deny himself and take up his cross daily and follow me. For whoever wants to save his life will lose it, but whoever loses his life for me will save it. What good is it for a man to gain the whole world, and yet lose or forfeit his very self"* (Luke 9:23-26)?

It was as if Jesus was saying in contemporary words, "Take up your electric chair and follow me." In those days, when a man took up his cross, it meant that he was not coming back. It was the end; and he was going to die. He had no more plans of his own.

The message of the New Testament is not "Jesus is the Answer". It's really "Jesus is Lord."

The following chart shows the difference between the true message of the New Testament versus one that is a partial and counterfeit message. NOTE: The benefits on the left side are all included on the right side. **The benefits come as a result of His Lordship.**[7]

---

[7] Commitment To A Local Expression of the Body of Christ, Larry Tomczak, 1978

This is born out in Scripture. For example: *"Bless the <u>Lord</u>, O my soul: and all that is within me, bless his holy name. Bless the <u>Lord</u>, O my soul, and forget not all his benefits: who forgiveth all thine iniquities; who healeth all thy diseases; who redeemeth thy life from destruction; who crowneth thee with loving kindness and tender mercies..."* (Psalm 103:1-4).

"The <u>Lord</u> is my shepherd, I shall not want..." (Psalm 23:1).

Counterfeit Gospel	Vs	**Authentic Gospel**
Come to Jesus and <u>GET</u>		Come to Jesus and <u>GIVE</u>
• Healed		• Your life to His control
• Joy & Peace		• Yourself as a living sacrifice
• Prosperity & Excitement		• Seek first the Kingdom of God and all things added to you
• Blessings		
I am Lord. Jesus is my servant		Jesus is Lord. I am His servant

When constructing a house, building an unstable foundation is not wise. This is also true of our spiritual lives. Jesus taught His disciples this truth with an illustration: *"Everyone who hears these sayings of Mine, and does not do them, will be like a foolish man who built his house on sand: and the rain descended, the floods came, and the winds blew and beat on that house; and it fell. And great was its fall"* (Matthew 7:26-27).

The shifting morals of our present world can be confusing. We may be tempted to let culture or the opinions of society be the foundation for the decisions we make. But obeying the unwavering truth of God's Word brings stability unavailable anywhere else. *"Therefore, whoever hears these sayings of Mine, and does them, I will liken him to a wise man who built his house on the rock"* (Matthew 7:24).[8]

So let's build our lives on the solid foundation by making Jesus Christ Lord and Owner of our hearts.

---

[8] Our Daily Bread, "Fault Line," Dennis Fisher, February 5, 2011

CHAPTER 5

CHANGE ALL THE LOCKS

What are the doors that open up your heart? What "buttons" can the enemy of our soul push in us to cause damage and destruction to occur in the Body of Christ? Do the "keys and locks" to the doors of our heart need to be changed? What kinds of things provoke us? Have we ever known or are we, ourselves, people like: Angela Angry, Aaron Arrogance, Evy Envy, Giddy Gossip, Rep Torn, and Sensitive Samantha? Hebrews 12: 1-2. Galatians 5: 13-22.

DO WE NEED TO CHANGE THE "LOCK" OF BITTERNESS AND UNFORGIVENESS (Ephesians 4:31-32)?

Sensitive Samantha was a young Christian who lived with a very abusive non-Christian husband. After many years of being instructed to "stay faithful", Sensitive Samantha found a caring pastor who ministered to her hurt. Ever since this experience, however, she has been super sensitive to the actions and responses of other Christians. She doubts their sincerity and avoids confiding in anyone. Whenever she perceives that someone is insensitive to her, she feels her only solution is to move to another church.

DO WE NEED TO CHANGE THE "LOCK" OF ENVY (1Peter 2:1)?

Evie Envy was a member of the ladies group at her church. Clear Lee Sincere was the leader. Evie Envy was jealous of Clear and had influence with the pastor's wife. She used this influence to get things done the way she wanted in the group. She took away some of the special heart-to-heart ministries that Clear Lee Sincere had instituted and also made the meetings much less nurturing than before. As a result, attendance became more forced than spontaneous. Clear Lee was hurt and suffered in silence through the rest of her term in office. She refused to run for leadership the following year, and Evie Envy became the new leader. Eventually the group dwindled and was abandoned.

DO WE NEED TO CHANGE THE "LOCK" OF PRIDE (1John 2:16)?

Aaron Arrogance was a wealthy church member. He used his money and his prosperous privately-owned business to exercise influence over the church. For example, as long as things were going his way, he would use men from his company to make repairs or paint the church. He also had his "own" friends in the church who he thought were worthy to associate with him and his family – others were excluded. If he took you out to lunch, it was only to get something from you that at the time he needed – like support for some election or issue. When he was unhappy about how the church board was spending money, he convinced the pastor and other church members to elect his son and a friend to the board so they could "fix" the problem. When the church decided to allow women to become deacons at an annual business meeting, Aaron Arrogance and his wife rudely left the church and never returned – embarrassing everyone and causing some young Christians to stumble in their faith.

Change All The Locks

DO WE NEED TO CHANGE THE "LOCK" OF SLANDER (Ephesians 4:31)?

Rep Torn was recently married. He needed a job to support his wife and a child they hoped to have some day. So Helpful Hand decided to intercede for him with a company that was doing work for Helpful Hand's employer. Because of his influence, they hired Rep Torn. Helpful Hand also arranged for another member of his church, Grateful Youth, to be hired. Rep Torn and Grateful Youth then worked together. Helpful Hand would give Rep Torn a ride to and from work whenever it was needed. He even gave him and his wife a vacation at his Summer house. Rep Torn was not very good at his job but his employer kept him on to show respect for Helpful Hand.

After a while, however, when there were cutbacks, Rep Torn and Grateful Youth had to be let go. Their employer, however, gave them plenty of notice to get other jobs. While they waited, Rep Torn began discrediting Helpful Hand's reputation to Grateful Youth – telling him how Helpful Hand wasn't doing enough for them, and saying other disparaging remarks.

After they were terminated, Rep Torn and Helpful Hand were in the back of the church. Rep Torn began blaming Helpful Hand for Grateful Youth not attending church any more. He became very loud – with many other church members around them – and said it was Helpful Hand who was responsible for this because he hadn't saved their jobs. Rep Torn became so emotional that some people went to get the pastor, who eventually had him come in for counseling. After that, Helpful Hand wondered if those who overheard the argument ever received his Sunday School teaching any more. Did they believe Rep Torn's slander?

DO WE NEED TO CHANGE THE "LOCK" OF ANGER (Colossians 3:8)?

Angela Angry was an African-American and resented the church Board for not removing the pastor who called her husband "boy." She disliked the pastor also because he was caught in an adulterous situation and was never disciplined. Angela Angry was very emotional and during Sunday morning service would usually verbalize her reactions to whatever the pastor would be preaching about. There was nothing against the pastor spoken at these times. Her comments, however, were loud enough at times for the whole church to hear and could be disruptive. One day, in the middle of his sermon, the pastor told Angela Angry to be quiet, pointing his finger at her from the pulpit. Instantly, she rose to her feet and angrily criticized the pastor before the entire congregation. Then she, her husband and daughter decisively left the church, still shouting at the pastor. Instead of taking her concerns to the church Board in a proper manner, that night, and for some time thereafter, Angela Angry made phone calls to other church members slandering the pastor and dredging up the pastor's past. As a result not only did her family leave the church but many others besides.

DO WE NEED TO CHANGE THE "LOCK" OF GOSSIP (Ephesians 4:29)?

Giddy Gossip didn't like the pastor's wife, Pure Lee, because she didn't fit the image of what a pastor's wife should be in Giddy Gossip's high-class township. Pure Lee was a real homemaker. She mended clothes. She canned vegetables. She also blanched vegetables and froze them so they would last for a year. She gave seminars to the women of the church on being a Biblical woman. She and the pastor were foster-parents to a dozen children – some of whom they had adopted. Many of them were problem children – both mentally and emotionally. When she wanted them home, Pure Lee would whistle for them and they would come to her. Giddy Gossip couldn't stand Pure Lee. She thought that Pure Lee wasn't what a "real Christian" wife should be like. So she criticized the pastor's wife every chance she got; and she overemphasized Pure Lee's weaknesses to others in the church. As a result, the other women wouldn't receive guidance from Pure Lee, and after only two years she and pastor were forced to leave the church.

OTHER "LOCKS" THAT NEED TO BE CHANGED

Roscoe Macho romances all the married women in the church.

Grey Betray pretends to be your friend until it's in his interest to betray your friendship.

Tammy Taker is so self-absorbed that she wants the pastor's attention and time on the smallest of matters.

Dizzy Disrespect publically voices his complaints about the pastor.

Reba Rebel leaves the church because the pastor or church board doesn't see things her way.

Wane Worth has a low self-esteem and feels that everyone is picking on her.

Pastor Patronize appears to be supporting and encouraging people, but isn't sincere and really only does it to keep people in the church.

Pastor Pushy is a micro-manager whose philosophy of management is "my way or the highway."

Pastor Compete sets up others who are effective in ministry as his competitors rather than encouraging them to be the best they can be for Christ.

Pastor Mule Driver likes the glory that comes from successful ministry but wants everyone else but himself to do the work.

IN CONTRAST TO ALL OF THIS

Jesus said, *"A new commandment I give you: Love one another. As I have loved you, so you must love one another. All men will know that you are my disciples if you love one another"* (John 13: 34-35). *"Let love be without hypocrisy. Abhor what is evil. Cling to what is good. Be kindly affectionate to one another with brotherly love, in honor giving preference to one another…"* (Romans 12:9-10).

So where necessary let's change the "locks" to the doors of our heart!

CHAPTER 6

TURN ON THE OUTSIDE LIGHTS

I just had some lights installed outside my house that automatically turn on when an object gets close enough to them. Not only are they very convenient, but they also deter people who might want to steal something or damage my property.

Are we letting the light of Christ shine through our lives? Are we living, breathing representations of the character and love of Christ? – *"not being conformed to this world's standards but transformed by the renewing of our minds"* (Romans 12:2).

SCRIPTURAL SUPPORT FOR LETTING OUR LIGHT SHINE

The following scriptures remind us that our good works help to shine the light of Christ on the distress, dissatisfaction, and darkness of the world around us:

"Let your light so shine before men, that they might see your good works, and give glory to your Father in heaven" (Matthew 5:16).

"For by grace you have been saved through faith, and that not of yourselves; it is the gift of God, not of works, lest anyone should boast. For we are His workmanship, created in Christ Jesus for

good works, which God prepared beforehand that we should walk in them" (Ephesians 2:8-10).

Good works demonstrate the reality of our faith – *"What good is it, my brothers, if a man claims to have faith but has no deeds? Can such faith save him?" "...faith without works is dead..."* (James 2:14, 26).

In Revelation 2:2, 9, 13, 19, Jesus tells us that He is well aware of our good deeds: *"I know thy works..."*

In Romans 13:11-14, the Apostle Paul tells us, *"Put on the armor of light..."*

1Timothy 6:18 instructs us to make our lives rich in good works.

1Peter 2:12 says that the unsaved should behold our good works and glorify our Father.

"Greater works than these shall thou do..." (John 14:12).

TO WHOM ARE OUR GOOD WORKS DIRECTED

As we run the Christian race, there are two groups of people around us. In the grandstands are those who are observing how we run. Our goal is to run so well that they will come out of the stands and join us in the race. Our good works help to show them the love of God in Christ. They demonstrate in a small way the sacrifice that our Lord endured to pay the debt for our sins that we could not pay – the judgment by God that he who sins must die. Jesus took that judgment by taking upon Himself all our sins and dying for us.

The second group of people around us, as we run the Christian race, is our teammates – our fellow runners. They have accepted Christ's sacrifice for them, and now are running the race of life

God's way. Our good works will encourage them to keep on running for the prize of the high calling of God in Christ Jesus. Philippians 3:14. Our good works will help them press forward to "gain Christ" – to become like Him! Philippians 3:8.

EXAMPLES OF GOOD WORKS TO THE UNSAVED COMMUNITY

Support the Salvation Army or other rescue missions with food, clothing, home furnishings.

Help at soup kitchens for the homeless.

Do missionary work at home and abroad.

Pray for neighbors, friends, family, and our coworkers.

Greet everyone with a smile and treat them with sensitivity and tenderness.

Restrain evil by being proactive. 2Thessalonians 2:7.

Lead them to Christ, and make them His disciples. Matthew 28:19. Use our testimony to tell them the good news of Christ's shed blood for them. Revelation 12:11.

Teach them the Word of God.

Be an example of Christ to them. Jesus is the Light of the world. We need to walk in the light as He is in the light so people will see Christ in us – the Hope of Glory.

EXAMPLES OF GOOD WORKS FOR THE BRETHREN

Obey the "one another" scriptures. There are about thirty of these scriptures in the New Testament. Here are several of them:

Restore one another in the spirit of meekness - Galatians 6:1

Serve one another – Galatians 5:13

Submit yourselves one to another – Ephesians 5:21

Pray for one another – Ephesians 6:18

Esteem (or prefer) the other better than ourselves – Philippians 2:3

Bear with one another and forgive one another – Colossians 3:1

Comfort one another – 2Corinthians 1:4

Meet the needs of one another – 1John 3:17

We should also watch carefully not to ambush one another by becoming an Angela Angry, Evy Envy, Rep Torn, Sensitive Samantha, Giddy Gossip, Aaron Arrogance, Roscoe Macho, etc. Romans 13:11-14 says, *"Put on the armor of light..."*

We should also seek the mind of Christ together for developing a strategic plan for our church. Philippians 2:2; Romans 15:5, 12:16.

WHAT DOES GOD REQUIRE?

What does God consider to be "good work," and what does He require of us: *"To do justly, to love mercy, and to walk humbly with our God"* (Micah 6:8). In addition, Jesus was confronted by people who had seen Him do the work of multiplying five loaves and two fish to feed about five thousand. They asked Him, *"What shall we do, that we might work the works of God?"* Jesus answered, *"This is the work of God, that you believe on him whom he has sent"* (John 6:29).

We need to let our light shine by embracing Christ's values found in the cross:

DO JUSTLY

This is all about righteousness. Jesus said, *"Seek first the kingdom of God and His righteousness..."* (Matthew 6:33). This "good work" is demonstrated as we embrace Christ's value to <u>Serve Others</u>. It is the self-sacrifice of the cross – John 3:16. We also demonstrate this work by embracing the <u>Wisdom From Above</u> which is *"first pure"* according to James 3:17. This is the holiness of the cross – 2Corinthians 5:21.

LOVE MERCY

To love mercy means to embrace Christ's value of being <u>Heart-to-Heart</u>. It's about caring enough to get to know others and let them know you. As we do this, the barriers between us are torn down in Christ, and we desire God's best for them. This is the love of the cross – Romans 5:8

WALK HUMBLY

Walking humbly with God means remembering that God is in control – not us. We are dependent on Him for everything, and because of that we don't twist others' arms or back them into a corner to "do things our way." We draw people to us – as Christ drew people to Himself. I like to call this value of Christ <u>Pull Don't Push</u>. It is the humility and obedience of the cross – Philippians 3:8

CHAPTER 7

GET YOUR WEAPONS OF PROTECTION READY

If we knew a thief was coming to our home, one of the things we would do is grab some weapon to protect ourselves and our friends and family with us. Spiritually, we have weapons given by God to defend ourselves from our enemy's tactics.

THE WEAPON OF THANKFULNESS

One of these weapons we've been given to ensnare the devil is thankfulness. The devil's deceit and trickery is foiled when we maintain an attitude of gratitude throughout our circumstances. God will turn the tables on him. He will be ambushed by God.

In 2 Chronicles 20, we find that the men of Ammon, Moab and Mount Seir were coming to drive the Israelites out of the possession (i.e. the land) God gave them as an inheritance. But Jehoshaphat, king of Judah, appointed men to sing to the Lord and to praise Him for the splendor of His holiness. As they went out at the head of the army, they said, *"Give thanks to the Lord, for His love endures forever"* (verse21). The next verse says, *"As they began to sing and praise, the Lord set <u>ambushes</u> against the men of Ammon and Moab and Mount Seir who were invading Judah, and they were defeated"* (verse 22). Let's praise God and ensnare the enemy of our soul.

EXHORTATIONS FROM SCRIPTURE

The Scripture is replete with exhortations to give thanks to the Lord. Here are several of them:

Deuteronomy 8:10. *"When you have eaten and are satisfied, praise the Lord your God for the good land he has given you."*

Psalm 100:4-5. *"Enter his gates with thanksgiving and his courts with praise; give thanks to him and praise his name. For the Lord is good and his love endures forever; his faithfulness continues through all generations."* Psalm 107:21-22. *"Let them give thanks to the Lord for his unfailing love and his wonderful deeds for men. Let them sacrifice thank offerings and tell of his works with songs of joy."*

Colossians 1:10-12. *"And we pray this in order that you may live a life worthy of the Lord and may please him in every way: bearing fruit in every good work, growing in the knowledge of God, being strengthened with all power according to his glorious might so that you may have great endurance and patience, and joyfully giving thanks to the Father, who has qualified you to share in the inheritance of the saints in the kingdom of light."* Note here that the Apostle Paul has made joyfully giving thanks in a Christian's life equal in importance with bearing fruit, growing to know God, and being strengthened with all power!

Colossians 3:13-15. *"Bear with each other and forgive whatever grievances you may have against one another. Forgive as the Lord forgave you. And over all these virtues put on love, which binds them all together in unity. Let the peace of Christ rule in your hearts, since, as members of one body, you were called to peace. And be thankful."* Here is a clear indication that being thankful helps us extend forgiveness to others and to maintain a clear channel for dispensing peace from our hearts.

1Thessalonians 5:18. *"Be joyful always; pray continually; give thanks in all circumstances, for this is God's will for you in Christ Jesus."*

INGRATITUDE WAS THE DEVIL'S DOWNFALL

Let's look at ingratitude for a moment. This was Satan's downfall – that's why he keeps trying to ambush us with the same attitude! Sometimes he gets us to be ungrateful by discouraging us in our circumstances – that's why we are moved by the Holy Spirit to *"encourage one another"* (1 Thessalonians 5:11). Sometimes he tries to separate us from the brethren through pride – that's why we are told, *"Brethren, if a man be overtaken in a fault, ye which are spiritual, restore such a one in the spirit of meekness..."* (Galatians 6:1).

Satan is an expert at these attitudes because it was ingratitude and pride that led to his ruin. He knows what happened to him because of being ungrateful to God and he wants to have the same thing happen to us. Lucifer (i.e. Satan) had so much to give thanks for but he refused. He was created to be beautiful with an internal ability for giving continuous praise to God through music – but instead of praising, he rebelled and desired the praise for himself that only God should receive. Here are the key scriptures:

Ezekiel 28: 12-17. *"...Thou sealest up the sum, full of wisdom, and perfect in beauty. Thou hast been in Eden the garden of God; every precious stone was thy covering, the sardius...the workmanship of thy tabrets and of thy pipes was prepared in thee in the day thou wast created. Thou are the anointed cherub that covereth (i.e. a guardian cherub); and I have set thee so: thou wast upon the holy mountain of God; thou hast walked up and down in the midst of the stones of fire. Thou wast perfect in thy ways from the day that thou wast created, till iniquity was found in thee...therefore I will cast thee as profane out of the mountain of God: I will destroy thee, O covering cherub, from the midst of the stones of fire. Thine heart was lifted up because of thy beauty, thou hast corrupted thy wisdom by reason of thy brightness: I will cast thee to the ground..."*

Isaiah 15:12-16. *"How art thou fallen from heaven O Lucifer, son of the morning! How art thou cut down to the ground, which didst weaken the nations! For thou hast said in thine heart, I will ascend into heaven, I will exalt my throne above the stars of God: I will sit also upon the mount of the congregation, in the sides of the north: I will ascend above the heights of the clouds: I will be like the most High. Yet thou shall be brought down to hell, to the sides of the pit. They that see thee shall narrowly look upon thee, and consider thee, saying, Is this the man that made the earth to tremble, that did shake kingdoms..."*

GOD'S VIEW OF THE UNGRATEFUL

Jesus was very disturbed with ingratitude. For example, in Luke 17: 11-19 ten men who had leprosy met Him. They called out and asked Jesus to heal them. Jesus told them to go show themselves to the priests. As they were going, all were healed. One of them, a Samaritan, when he saw that he was healed, returned to thank Christ. Then Jesus asked, *"Were not all ten cleansed? Where are the other nine? Was no one found to return and give praise to God except this foreigner?"*

There are two points here: First, everyone should have returned to give thanks. Second, those who were "His people" should have been the first ones to give thanks! God will resist those who are ungrateful (i.e. too proud to say thanks). But He will give grace (i.e. unmerited favor) to the humble and thankful. James 4:6; 1 Peter 5:5.

Therefore, the Church needs to take an extra measure of Vitamin E (i.e. the Exalt Vitamin) – especially the nutrient of thanksgiving. The Apostle Peter gives a four-fold reason for giving thanks: *"But you are a chosen people, a royal priesthood, a holy nation, a people belonging to God, that you may declare the praises of him who called you out of darkness into his wonderful light"* (1 Peter 2:9).

So let's remember to be thankful in all our circumstances.

THE ARMOR OF GOD

Our Lord has given us other weapons of spiritual warfare that we should be using. The book of Ephesians calls these "the whole armor of God." *"Be strong in the Lord and in the power of His might. Put on the whole armor of God, that you may be able to stand against the wiles of the devil. For we do not wrestle against flesh and blood, but against principalities, against powers, against the rulers of the darkness of this age, against spiritual hosts of wickedness in the heavenly places."*

"Therefore take up the whole armor of God, that you may be able to withstand in the evil day, and having done all, to stand. Stand therefore, having girded your waist with truth, having put on the breastplate of righteousness, and having shod your feet with the preparation of the gospel of peace; above all, taking the shield of faith with which you will be able to quench all the fiery darts of the wicked one. And take the helmet of salvation, and the sword of the Spirit, which is the word of God; praying always with all prayer and supplication in the Spirit, being watchful to this end with all perseverance and supplication for all the saints...." (Ephesians 6:10-18).

WHAT IS THE ARMOR OF GOD?

The armor of God reminds me of another safety measure people use to keep themselves and their family safe from predators who would break into their homes. They build special rooms known as "safe rooms." If there's an intruder, the head of household ushers his family into the "safe room" to prevent any injury to his loved ones.

God's armor brings victory because it is much more than a protective covering. It is the very life of Jesus Christ Himself. *"Put on the armor,"* wrote Paul in his letter to the Romans, *"...clothe yourselves with the Lord Jesus Christ"* (Romans 13:12-14). When you do, He becomes your hiding place, your shelter, your "safe room" in the storm -- just as He was to David. Hidden in Him, you can count on His victory, for He not only covers you as a shield, He also fills you with His life.

"I am the vine; you are the branches," said Jesus. *"If a man **abides in Me** and **I in him**, he will bear much fruit; apart from me you can do nothing"* (John 15:5). Psalm 46:1 tells us that *"God is our refuge and strength."*

Jesus is our refuge because it is of God that we are in Christ. 1Corinthians 1:30. Since we are in Christ, everything He did became ours – His death, resurrection and ascension to the Father's right hand. We are spiritually already citizens of heaven. If there's a bookmark in a book and that book is sent to a foreign country, where does the bookmark go? Of course, it goes with the book. And so it is with us and Christ. He's the book and we are the bookmark. Wherever the book goes, so does the bookmark.

Jesus is our covering – put on Christ (our refuge). He is the whole armor of God. Jesus' Body was broken so we could enter in and become part of His Body. We have entered His wounds and are covered by His blood that cleanses us from all sin. And now if we sin, He can be (and is) faithful and just to forgive our sin and cleanse us from all unrighteousness. 1John 1:9. *"He who knew no sin, became sin for us so we could become the righteousness of God in Him"* (2Corinthians 5:21).

Since living in the safety of the armor means oneness with Jesus, we can expect to share His struggles as well as His peace. Remember, God offers us His victory in the midst of trouble -- not the absence of pain. Therefore, *"Do not be surprised at the painful trial you are suffering, as though something strange were happening to you, but rejoice that you participate in the sufferings of Christ..."* (1 Peter 4:12-13). Jesus said, *"In the world you shall have tribulation: but be of good cheer; I have overcome the world"* (John 16:33).

Committed Christians who face torture for their faith continue to testify to the supernatural strength - even joy - that enables them to endure unthinkable pain. They affirm with Paul, *"that in all these things we are more than conquerors through him who loved us.... For I am convinced that neither death nor life, neither angels nor demons, neither the present nor the future, nor any powers.... will be able to separate us from the love of God that is in Christ Jesus our Lord"* (Romans 8:37-39).

This wonderful truth has become reality to all who believe and follow Jesus. When you put on His armor, His life surrounds you and keeps you safe in Him. He is your precious friend, and you are His! So *"put on Christ"* (Galatians 3:27). He is your victory!

HOW DO WE "PUT ON" GOD'S ARMOR?

This life in Christ begins with knowing and trusting each part of the armor. The first part is TRUTH -- God's revelation of all that He is to us, all that He has done for us, and all that He promises to do for us in the days ahead. This wonderful, everlasting TRUTH is **written** in the Bible, **revealed** by the Holy Spirit, and **realized** through Jesus Christ.[9]

It cuts through all the world's distortions, deceptions, and compromises. When you study, memorize, live, and follow

---

[9] Adapted from The Armor of God, www.crossroad.to/Victory/Armor.htm

TRUTH, He enables you to see the world from God's high vantage point. For He is the TRUTH! Putting on the first piece of the armor means feeding on truth through daily Bible reading and making it part of you.

WHAT ARE THE PRACTICAL APPLICATIONS?

Belt of TRUTH - The belt is foundational for battle. It supported the weapons that allowed the soldier to fight. To win our spiritual battles our fight must be anchored to the truth found in Jesus alone. John 14:6.

Breastplate of RIGHTEOIUSNESS - The breastplate's function was to protect the vital organs. In close hand-to-hand combat, the breastplate was essential for survival. If we start to believe that our own righteousness, effort, or good works can make us worthy of God's protection, the advantage shifts to our enemy. We need to get our eyes off ourselves and back onto the provision of the cross and the righteousness found in our relationship with Christ. 2 Corinthians 5:21.

Shoes of READINESS AND PEACE – Without his sandals, a soldier was not prepared to fight and could easily be defeated. Our preparation for battle is the Gospel of Jesus' life, death, and resurrection. The work of Jesus here on earth brought us peace with God. This allows us to fight with boldness, confidence, perseverance, and peace. Isaiah 26: 3-4.

Shield of FAITH – Jesus is the focus of our faith. The only protection from the flaming arrows that rained down from the sky in ancient warfare was the shield. If dropped it was useless and the soldier's fate rested with himself. We trust Jesus alone as our shield. We can't rely on our abilities in the battle. Psalm 33: 20-22.

Helmet of SALVATION – The word "salvation" means "total deliverance". In Jesus, we can find deliverance in every situation: spiritual, emotional, and physical. He must be our Source, our Guide, our Way Out. We cannot deliver ourselves. Also, the helmet protects the mind that is being used by God to transform us into Christ's image. Romans 12: 1-2.

SWORD OF THE SPIRIT which is THE WORD OF GOD – Jesus is the Word of God made flesh. When used at close range by a skilled soldier, the sword was a deadly weapon. The Word is the written picture of Jesus. He is the living version of everything God wanted to say to mankind. The Word is a powerful weapon when used under the Spirit's power and direction. John 1:14.

CHAPTER 8

MAKE SURE YOU HAVE AN ESCAPE PLAN

Some people who live in multi-story houses keep a rope ladder under their beds as a means of escape in case of a fire or intruder. As mentioned earlier, other households maintain a "safe room" or "panic room" to keep their family secure.

BEFORE WE COME TO CHRIST

Everyone is running on one of two race tracks of life. They each have different finish lines – one leads to heaven and eternal life. The other leads to hell and destruction. Matthew 7:13-14. At any time in the course of our lives we can choose the track where we want to run. Before coming to Christ, the roar of the crowd (i.e. the world) not only creates the standards for living and being successful, but it also causes us to delude ourselves into thinking that we are something that we are really not. We run around in this cloud of darkness. What we see is sadly not what's really there – we are figuratively blind to what is real – to what is true. We lie to ourselves and/or call our sins something that makes them sound "right for the new millennium."

Selfish and evil people call themselves generous and good. Those in bondage to sin call themselves liberated. Those enjoying the folly of fools call themselves enlightened, and the lustful describe their sinful acts as love affairs.

It's as if we see the world upside down. Not only do we believe that we are the most important person in the world – and that we must take care of "me" first – but we also believe that the world is there for our benefit – to serve us. Our life becomes a journey of seeing how much we can take from what's there – to possess whatever the roar of the crowd has convinced us is most important to have.

If we were to remain in that state of mind, the end of our journey would land us in Hell – and, while there, we'd probably complain about how unfairly such a victorious champion like ourselves was being treated. Isaiah 5:20 warns us, *"Woe to those who call evil good and good evil."*

Thank God, that He is Light and there is no darkness in Him. *"His Word is a lamp unto our feet and a light unto our path"* (Psalm 119:105). Thank God, that He desires that no one should perish and that everyone should come to know the Truth. HE HAS PROVIDED AN ESCAPE PLAN SO THE REAL THIEF OF OUR SOULS – THE DEVIL - WILL NOT BE ABLE TO ROB AND DESTROY US (John 10:10).

He doesn't want anyone to remain wandering in that cloud of darkness. He has provided a way for every man, woman, and child to come out of the darkness and get onto the real race track of life that leads to eternal life. Jesus said, *"I am come that they might have life, and that they might have it more abundantly"* (John 10:10). Thank God for creating an inner voice in each of us called a conscience. And thank Him for crises in life that make us wonder whether we are really as successful as we think.

GETTING ON THIS REAL RACE TRACK

Getting "on track" with God involves the acceptance by faith of the following truths: <u>We are lost and cannot help ourselves out of our dilemma.</u>

"There is none righteous, no, not one" (Romans 3:10). *"All we like sheep have gone astray; we have turned everyone to his own way..."* (Isaiah 53:6). All our righteousness (i.e. "right living") is as filthy rags to God, who is pure holiness. Isaiah 64:6. *"For all have sinned and come short of the glory of God"* (Romans 3:23).

"Your iniquities [i.e. sins] have separated between you and your God, and your sins have hid his face from you..." (Isaiah 59:2). *"Wherefore, as by one man (i.e. Adam) sin entered into the world, and death by sin; and so death passed upon all men, for that all have sinned"* (Romans 5:12).

But, there is a solution – Christ is the escape plan:

"But God commends his love toward us, in that, while we were yet sinners Christ died for us" (Romans 5:8).

"For there is one God, and one mediator between God and men, the man Christ Jesus; who gave himself a ransom for all..." (1Timothy 2:5-6).

"For the wages of sin is death; but the gift of God is eternal life through Jesus Christ our Lord" (Romans 6:23).

"Ye were... redeemed with the precious blood of Christ, as of a lamb without blemish and without spot" (1Peter 1:18-19).

"For whosoever shall call upon the name of the Lord shall be saved" (Romans 10:13).

"If thou shalt confess with thy mouth the Lord Jesus and shalt believe in thine heart that God hath raised him from the dead, thou shalt be saved" (Romans10:9).

"For with the heart man believeth unto righteousness; and with the mouth confession is made unto salvation... Whosoever believeth on him shall not be ashamed" (Romans 10: 10-11).

WHEN WE ACCEPT THESE TRUTHS

Man is created in God's image. He is a triune being.

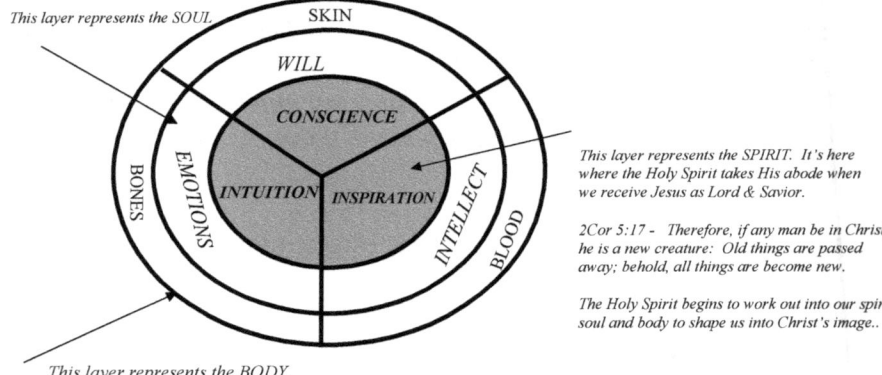

When we accept these truths, confess our sin with godly sorrow, determine to forsake sin, and sincerely ask Jesus to be our Savior and Lord, we are "receiving Jesus" and are "born-again"- literally "born from above". John 1: 10-13 says that Jesus came unto his own and his own received him not. But to all those who received him, he gave them the power to become children of God – even those who believe in His name – who were born not of blood, nor the will of man, but born of God (i.e. born from above or born-again).

We then enter the family of God and (just like blood is common in earthly family members) God sends His Holy Spirit to take up residence in all believers (i.e. members of God's spiritual family).

We are Christians only when we have received Christ and are born again. *"Verily, verily, I say unto thee, except a man be born* *again, he cannot see the kingdom of God"* (John 3:3)

THE RESURRECTION GIVES MEANING TO THE CROSS

The Bible tells us that Elijah was taken alive up to heaven in a whirlwind. 2 Kings 2:11. The most powerful reason, however, to believe in heaven and life after death is the resurrection of Christ. It was witnessed by hundreds. 1Corinthians 15:3-7. Though we sense in ourselves that life must be more than just our existence here, Jesus proved once for all that there is life after death.

The death of Christ is terrible news if it ends there. But because of His resurrection, it is "good news." It assures us that His work is finished – <u>that Christ atoned for everyone's sins. It also assures us that His work was perfect and that God was satisfied with His sacrifice</u> – that Jesus was the "propitiation" for our sins. That means Jesus appeased the wrath of God because of His anger against sin. God, The Father, demonstrated His satisfaction and confirmed Christ's work on the cross to atone for sin by raising Him from the dead. Acts 13:32-33.

Jesus said, *"I am the resurrection, and the life: he that believeth in me though he were dead, yet shall he live: And whosoever that liveth and believeth in me shall never die"* (John 11:25-26). Salvation – the escape plan - for you and me only requires our repentance of what we have done and our acceptance of what Christ has done for us. We *"call upon the name of the Lord."* God hears the cry of our repentant heart for forgiveness and "remembers" the work of His Son on our behalf. Our name is then written in heaven in the Lamb's book of ***life***. Luke 10:20; Revelation 21:27.

WHAT ABOUT THE CHRISTIAN WHO SINS? WHAT'S HIS ESCAPE PLAN?

When the five foolish virgins of Matthew 25: 1-13 realized that they had not prepared for the bridegroom's coming, they turned to the wise virgins to absolve them of their irresponsibility. *"The foolish ones said to the wise, 'Give us some of your oil; our lamps are going out'"* (v7). They needed to be accountable for their own actions. Jesus said, *"Not everyone who says to me, 'Lord, 'Lord,' will enter the kingdom of heaven, but only he who does the will of my Father who is in heaven"* (Matthew 7:21).

When we are "born-again", we are not only "saved" from the death sentence, but also delivered from the power of sin, itself. We are no longer in bondage to serve sin. We are set free to seek the kingdom of God and His righteousness. The "old man" in us that made us slaves to sin – that caused us to enjoy sinning – that convinced us that there was nothing wrong with what we were doing – is crucified with Christ. Romans 6:6.

When We Are Born-Again, The Old Man In Us Is Crucified With Christ

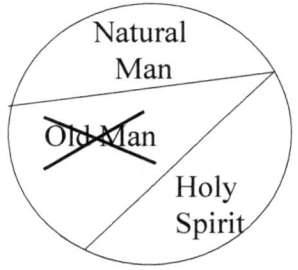

GOD, sending His Holy Spirit to dwell within us, gives us the power to overcome the temptation and attraction of sin and instead to produce pure "fruit". *"For when ye were servants of sin, ye were free from righteousness. What fruit had ye then in those things whereof ye are now ashamed? For the end of those things is death. But now being made free from sin, and become servants of God, ye have your fruit unto holiness, and the end everlasting life"* (Romans 6:20-22). *"...greater is He that is in you, than he that is in the world"* (1John 4:4).

That doesn't mean that we never sin – because our natural man is still alive in us. It means, however, that when we sin the Holy Spirit is faithful to convict us – so that we want to tell God we're

Make Sure You Have An Escape Plan   67

sorry for it, and affirm that we will turn from it. And then because of Christ's sacrifice for our sin, He (can now be and) is *"faithful and just to forgive our sins and to cleanse us from all unrighteousness"* (1John 1:9).   And **in faith**, we take God at His word that our sins are forgiven. F.A.I.T.H – Forsaking All I Trust Him.   That is GOD'S ESCAPE PLAN for when we sin as Christians.

remember...

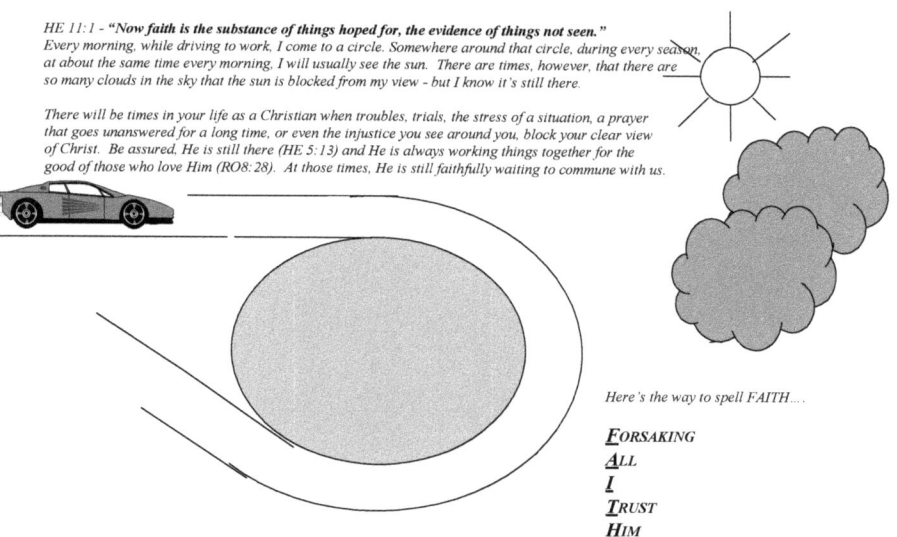

HE 11:1 - *"Now faith is the substance of things hoped for, the evidence of things not seen."*
Every morning, while driving to work, I come to a circle. Somewhere around that circle, during every season, at about the same time every morning, I will usually see the sun. There are times, however, that there are so many clouds in the sky that the sun is blocked from my view - but I know it's still there.

There will be times in your life as a Christian when troubles, trials, the stress of a situation, a prayer that goes unanswered for a long time, or even the injustice you see around you, block your clear view of Christ. Be assured, He is still there (HE 5:13) and He is always working things together for the good of those who love Him (RO 8:28). At those times, He is still faithfully waiting to commune with us.

Here's the way to spell FAITH....

*FORSAKING
ALL
I
TRUST
HIM*

GOD'S GRACE

The Apostle Paul wrote, *"For it is by grace you have been saved, through faith – and this not from yourselves, it is the gift of God – not by works, so that no one can boast"* (Ephesians 2:8-9). It's difficult for us humans to understand God's grace. Grace means "unmerited favor."   Some have said G.R.A.C.E means God's Riches At Christ's Expense. Grace is the distance between light and dark. It's the distance between perfect and imperfect. It's the distance between holiness and sin. It's the distance that Christ had to travel to pay the debt caused by our sin!

CHAPTER 9

THE "THIEF" COMES IN THE TWINKLING OF AN EYE

When the thief breaks into a house, there's no announcement – no warning – of his approach. He has probably surveyed the house for some time to know your habits so he can use the element of surprise. He uses the landscape around the house to hide himself. When he believes the moment is right, he makes his move to enter.

HOW WILL WE GET TO HEAVEN?

In John 11: 25-26, Jesus says, *"...I am the resurrection and the life. He who believes in me will live, even though he dies; and whoever lives and believes in me shall never die..."* What did He mean that we would live when we die, and then that if we live we would never die? I believe Jesus was speaking about the two ways we get to heaven.

In the first case, when we physically die we will have eternal life with Him and therefore will live even though we die. He came to give us this eternal life. We were under the sentence of death, but by His sacrifice that penalty was paid because He became the propitiation for our sins (i.e. the sacrifice pleasing to the Father).

In the second case, whoever is physically living and believing in Christ when He returns for us will never die. Those of us who are alive when Jesus returns, will be taken like Elijah was taken from the earth – we will never die. 2Kings 9-11. We call that experience The Rapture of the Church: 1Thessalonians 4: 15-17 says, *"According to the Lord's own word, we tell you that we who are still alive, who are left till the coming of the Lord, will certainly not precede those who have fallen asleep. For the Lord Himself will come down from heaven, with a loud command, with the voice of the archangel and with the trumpet call of God, and the dead in Christ will rise first.* ***After that, we who are still alive and are left will be caught up with them in the clouds to meet the Lord in the air. And so we will be with the Lord forever…"***

That's the event Jesus spoke about in John 14: 1-3, *"Do not let your hearts be troubled. Trust in God; trust also in me. There are many rooms in my Father's house; otherwise, I would have told you. I am going there to prepare a place for you. And if I go and prepare a place for you, I will come back and take you to be with me that you also may be where I am."*

Just like a thief in the night, this return of Christ will not be announced. It will be very sudden. I believe the archangel Michael (Daniel 12:1), who is the great prince and commander in God's army, will give a shout. He will declare that the enemy forces – the prince of the power of the air with all his demons – are sufficiently engaged and prevented from interfering. The trumpet call of God will signal that the angelic harvesters should reap the earth of His people. And in about $1/20^{th}$ of a second – in the twinkling of an eye – all believers in Christ will be given resurrection bodies and will vanish from the earth.

1Corinthians 15:51-58 says, *"Listen, I tell you a mystery: We shall not all sleep, but we shall all be changed – in a flash, in the twinkling of an eye, at the last trumpet. For the trumpet will sound, the dead will be raised imperishable, and we shall be changed. For the perishable must clothe itself with the imperishable, and the mortal with immortality...Therefore, my dear brothers, stand firm. Let nothing move you. Always give yourselves fully to the work of the Lord, because you know that your labor in the Lord is not in vain."*

FINALLY HOME

Many people have come into New York harbor to catch their first glimpse of lady liberty. Fifty years ago, the trip might have taken eleven days and was of the "no-frill" variety. The travelers were probably sea sick from stormy seas and home sick for friends and family left behind. Before they set out, they decided to endure whatever hardships that were required to make America their home – and be free at last – home at last!

This life can be like a stormy sea voyage. Everyone who lives is on some ship that they have chosen to board. Jesus said that straight is the road and narrow is the gate that leads to eternal life in heaven; but broad is the way and wide is the gate that leads to destruction. Matthew 7: 13-14. Everyone boards through some gate. Jesus said that He was the gate of the sheepfold. John 10:7-9. He is the pearl of great price out of which each gate in the heavenly Jerusalem is made. Revelation 21:21. He is the only way into heaven. Jesus said, *"I am the Way, the Truth, and the Life. No one goes to the Father except by Me* (John 14:6)*."*

Everyone is on some ship. As long as we live, we are free to do whatever we like on the ship or to choose to leave one ship for another. We might make choices that make us rich or poor, happy or sad, popular or unpopular. The most important choice, however, is the choice of ship. Because every ship has an itinerary set by God.

Someday, those who have lived their lives without Christ – who have never received Him as their Lord and Savior – will arrive at a destination of death and destruction. Romans 3:10, 23; 5:12; 6:23.

They will find themselves in Hell, and then later, after the Great White Throne Judgment, in the lake of fire and brimstone that was originally prepared for Satan and the rebellious angels. Revelation 20: 10-15.

Someday, those of us who have trusted Jesus as our personal Savior and Lord will leave this life and go to the place he has prepared for us in heaven. John 14:1-3. The journey here may be difficult and uncomfortable – the sea we're in might be full of furious storms – but we look forward to the final destination. One look at His dear face, all sorry will erase. *"I consider that our present sufferings are not worth comparing with the glory that will be revealed in us"* (Romans 8:18).

Think about Jesus' journey (*"who for the joy that was set before him, endured the cross, despising the shame..."* (Hebrews 12:2). He was hated by the religious establishment; betrayed by a trusted disciple (John 13:21); disowned by his closest ally (John 13:38); and, abandoned by all His chosen apostles (John 16:31-32). The people he had helped who cried out "Hosanna" on Sunday, cried out "Crucify him" on Friday. John 19: 14-16. Finally, He was flogged and then crucified. John 19:1, 17-19.

We're told to run patiently the race set before us (the journey) looking unto Jesus (and his journey). Hebrews 12:1-2.

A Christian's ship on the journey of life has three stops from here to eternity. Accepting Jesus as Savior and Lord, we **are saved**. Nothing we could ever do would warrant our being saved. Only Christ's work on the cross for us can pay the price for our salvation. It's a gift of God. Ephesians 2: 8-10. But that's only the first stop.

The next stop takes the rest of our lives – we **are being saved**. Sometimes this stop is called Sanctification. 2Timothy 2:21. It's getting rid of all the carnal character qualities, priorities, and behaviors we brought with us when we accepted Christ as Savior and Lord. Luke 5:36-39; Acts 10. It's putting on Christ! It's being separated *from* the world and *to* God. Remember one of the previous chapters entitled **Take Inventory of All Your Household Goods**. Remember, our good works don't save us (Ephesians 2:8-9) but we do have a job to do here on earth. As believers, we are *"created in Christ Jesus for good works"* (2:10).

The next stop is heaven – we experience **the result of our salvation.**

A TASTE OF THINGS TO KNOW ABOUT HEAVEN

It's impossible for a telescope to see where heaven is. But it's possible for us to hear a call from heaven and for heaven to hear us. Remember Hagar and her son. It says that God heard the voice of the lad and an angel called to Hagar out of heaven. Genesis 21:17. Also, when Abraham was sacrificing Isaac, an angel called to him out of heaven. Genesis 22:12.

Some astronomers have found a section in space in the direction of the North Star that looks like a big hole in space. It's surrounded by a glow of light and it can fit thirty of our own solar systems in it. Could that be where heaven is? Ezekiel 1:4; Psalm 75:6. We know heaven is up. Here are just a few verses:

When Jesus left earth, He went up. Acts 1: 9-10.

Elijah was brought up to heaven by a whirlwind. 2 Kings 2:11.

After Ezekiel was visited by God, He was lifted up out of sight. Ezekiel 1:4; 11:24.

John saw the heavenly Jerusalem coming down from heaven. See Revelation chapter 21.

Psalm 103:11 says, *"For as the heaven is <u>high above the earth</u>, so great is His mercy to them that fear Him."*

Did you know that Paul talked about going to the third heaven? The first heaven is where the birds and planes fly. The second heaven is the celestial space where the sun, moon, and planets are. The third heaven is where Paul was, where God has His throne and where the New Jerusalem is, as well as all those who have died in Christ before us. Acts 14:19-20; 2Corinthians 12:2-4; Revelation 21 and 22.

Our trials and suffering now are not worthy to be compared with what God has prepared for us. Romans 8:18. *"Eye hath not seen, nor ear heard, nor has it entered into the heart of man, the things which God has prepared for those who love him"* (1 Corinthians 2:9).

SETTING YOUR GLOBAL POSITIONING SYSTEM (GPS)

After speaking to His disciples about preparing a place for them in heaven and coming back for them (John 14:1-3), Jesus added, *"You know where I am going and you know the way"* (vs. 4). Thomas then answered what every man's heart cry is, *"We don't know where you're going, so how can we know the way?"* (vs. 5). Jesus told him, *"I am the way, the truth, and the life: no man goes to the Father except by me"* (vs. 6).

But Jesus also said, *"Not everyone who says to me, Lord, Lord will enter the kingdom of heaven, but only he who **does the will of my Father** who is in heaven. Many will say on that day, Lord, Lord, did we not prophesy in your name, and in your name drive out demons and do many miracles? Then I will tell them plainly, 'I never knew you. Away from me, you evildoers'"* (Matthew 7:21-23)!

What does doing the will of the Father in heaven mean? John 6:28-29 says, *"Then they asked him, 'What shall we do to do the work of God?' Jesus answered, 'The work of God is **to believe in the one who he has sent.**'"* It means believing who Jesus is (God come in the flesh); believing what He says (the Word of God); and with sincere hearts, trusting and obeying His Word.

It also means letting your light shine among men, that they may see your good works and glorify your Father in heaven as Jesus told us. It's like creating a bank account in heaven that contains the people you touched in some way for Christ by emulating him as the Light of the World and as the Servant of all! Matthew 5:14-16. Remember, he said, *"Where your treasure is your heart will be also"* (Matthew 6:19-21).

WHAT WILL WE DO IN HEAVEN?

Here are some of the activities we look forward to in heaven:

We will worship the Lord

We will be reunited with loved ones and bring each other up-to-date.

We will learn to live in our new (immortal) bodies and travel the universe.

We will learn from fathers of the faith (e.g. Have you ever wondered what Samson saw in Delilah?)

We will learn from the Lord to rule & reign with Him forever.

We will feel the joy of youth again –never feel tired, weary, or old again as we drink from the river that proceeds from God's throne.

And much, much more. Remember, *"Eye hath not seen, nor ear heard, nor has it entered into the heart of man, the things which God has prepared for those who love him"* (1 Corinthians 2:9).

Here are some of the major events we look forward to when we get to heaven. They are described in the chapters to follow:

The Judgment Seat of Christ (2Corinthians 5:10)

The Marriage Supper of the Lamb (Revelation 19: 6-9)

The Battle of Armageddon (Revelation 19:11-21)

Rule & Reign with Jesus for a thousand years on the earth (Luke 19: 11-26)

The New Jerusalem (1 Corinthians 3:12-14; 1Peter 1:7; Revelation 21:19-20)

CHAPTER 10

THE "THIEF" BECOMES OUR JUDGE - THE JUDGMENT SEAT OF CHRIST

"Know ye not that they which run in a race run all, but one receiveth the prize? So run, that ye may obtain. And every man that striveth for the mastery is temperate in all things. Now they do it to obtain a corruptible crown; but we an incorruptible [one]" (1Corinthians 9:24).

We've been speaking about preparing ourselves for Christ's return. Jesus gave us a metaphor to help us get ready. He told us to prepare like we would if we knew a thief in the night would be coming to break into our home. We're not privileged most of the time in knowing a future event – the future is hidden from us. But God has been gracious by giving us His Word to see just far enough ahead to help us live His way, and be prepared for Christ. His Word is like our automobile headlights. They can't illuminate the entire road for us, but they give us enough light to keep us moving forward – and to keep us away from the obstacles and out of the ditches.

The One who told us to prepare for Him to come *"like a thief in the night"* is Himself preparing to judge our Christian lives. Seeing the future Judgment Seat of Christ, albeit through a glass darkly, helps us better prepare to see Christ.

A JUDGMENT THAT BRINGS REWARDS

God gives us many new starts – there are many "start lines" in the Christian race. Whenever we stumble and fall, (i.e. when we fall short of God's expectations of us), we confess our sin to Him and because Christ has already paid the penalty for that sin, we get a new start (1John 1:9). That new start line isn't back at the beginning, however, it is right where we stumbled – we keep going forward from there.

Yes, there are many start lines as we run for our life God's way, but there is only one finish line. It's at the Judgment Seat of Christ where all Christians together must appear. *"For we must all appear before the judgment seat of Christ; that every one may receive the things done in his body, according to that he hath done, whether it be good or bad"* (2Corinthians 5:10). At the finish line, there will be crowns given as rewards for what we did to cooperate with the Holy Spirit here on earth. These crowns will go to those who, through the power of the Holy Spirit, build *"gold, silver and precious stones"* upon the foundation of Christ. To those who work in their own strength, those works will be burned up and considered *"wood, hay, and stubble."* 1Corinthians 3:11-15.

There are five crowns given in the Word of God as follows:

- "Crown of life" for those withstanding tribulation (Revelation 2:10)
- "Crown of glory" for elders, pastors, and leaders who have oversight of God's flock (1Peter 5:1-4)
- "Crown of rejoicing" for faithfully witnessing (1Thessalonians 2:19)
- "Crown of righteousness" for those who long for Christ's return (2Timothy 4:8)

- "Incorruptible crown" for victors of the daily spiritual struggles (1Corinthians 9:25)

In Revelation 4:10, we have a picture of the twenty-four elders having crowns on their heads. This means that the Judgment Seat of Christ had taken place. They took their crowns and cast them at the foot of the throne saying, *"Thou art worthy, O Lord, to receive glory and honor and power: for thou hast created all things and for thy pleasure they are and were created."* So we, likewise, who receive one or more crowns will cast them at the feet of Christ. That's why when Christ returns (with us) in Revelation 19:12, He has on His head *"many crowns."*

So then, if we don't wear the crowns we receive at the Judgment Seat of Christ, what do we wear throughout eternity? Daniel 12:3 has the answer. It says, *"And they that be wise shall shine as the brightness of the firmament; and they that turn many to righteousness as the stars forever and ever."* We won't have crowns. We'll wear a mantle of light – similar to the Mount of Transfiguration light Christ showed to Peter, James and John. Matthew 17:2. I believe the degree of radiance – like different stars shine brighter than others – will be based upon our faithfulness to follow the Holy Spirit's guidance on earth.

RUNNING THE RACE OF LIFE GOD'S WAY

Before discussing this finish line any further, let's reflect upon some things about this Christian race. Every Christian is a spiritual athlete. We are running for our life God's way. At first we were influenced by the "roar of the crowd" – the world, flesh, and the devil. We were on the broad track that was leading us to spiritual death. The Father's heart was broken because we, whom He had created to enjoy His fellowship, had an estranged relationship with Him because of sin.

He sent His Son, who took upon Himself the form of a servant and was made in the likeness of men. He humbled Himself and, as an obedient Son, became the sacrifice for our sins that satisfied the Father. All of us who receive Christ are then "born-again" (i.e. born from above) by the Holy Spirit, who takes up residence within us. He sets us into the kingdom of God, which is both invisible (i.e. within us) and visible (i.e. in the form of the church).

Even though we are born-again, however, we find that the old values and behaviors that we acquired from the "roar of the crowd" continue with us. Over time we experience a transformation of these values and behaviors. We find the natural man in us, who competes with Christ in us, being reduced to zero – wrestled to the ground. Genesis 32:24-30. This happens as we discipline ourselves to regularly study the Word of God, worship Him, fellowship with other believers, pray to our Father, surrender ourselves for His service, and by suffering trials/tribulations with His companionship and comfort.

By waiting upon the Lord to continually renew our strength, we run with patience and endure the "muscle aches" that of necessity come with long distance running. We maintain a portrait of the Lord before us. We don't just run for Him but from Him – He must do the work because anything done in our own strength (i.e. the natural man) can't satisfy Him. We *see* Him as our Inspiration (i.e. the Great Initiator of our faith), our Role Model, who's already run this race, and our divine Coach, who first teaches us how to run and then perfects us so we run well.

WITH THE HELP OF THE HOLY SPIRIT

We are gently drawn onward by the Holy Spirit, who is always there reminding us of the race we are running:

Because our enemy Satan is a liar and attempts to deceive Christians concerning what the real abundant Christian life is all about, the Holy Spirit asks, "What track are you on?" Is it the "great career track?" Is it the "ego building track?" Is it the "material possessions or investment track?" "Or are you", He reminds us, "on the high-calling track?" This is the narrow track – the course that's marked out by the example of Christ and leads to being shaped into His image. Philippians 3:14.

The Holy Spirit asks, "Is Jesus Lord of your life? Does He own the deed to your heart or is He just a guest there?"

He asks, "What equipment are you wearing?" Is it the armor of God that includes having *"our feet shod with the preparation of the gospel of peace"* (Ephesians 6:15); or are we wearing shoes with pointed tips that hurt our fellow runners?

The racetrack is full of obstacles – many peaks and valleys – many things that cause runners to stumble, scrap their arms and legs. The Holy Spirit reminds us that Jesus never leaves or forsakes us. He will not let us go through any suffering without Him. He's the one who asks us to come unto Him when we labor and are heavy-laden, to learn of Him, because He is meek and lowly of heart and will give us rest. Matthew 11:28.

The Holy Spirit asks us, "How are you running – by faith or by sight?" *"Without faith it is impossible to please him: for he that cometh to God must believe that he is, and that he is a rewarder of them that diligently seek him"* (Hebrews 11:6). He reminds us that *"All things work together for good to them that love God, to them who are the called according to his purpose"* (Romans 8:28).

How are you moving? Are you crawling, walking, or running when it comes to Christian growth? Runners kick hardest when they "see" the finish line. You may be crawling and not running well because you have a "fuzzy" view of the finish line.

Has the Holy Spirit ever asked you about who wins this Christian race? Do you try to beat me to the finish line? Do Christians compete with each other to win? No, that should never be the case. This is a team race where we all win together! We finish the race together and we are always about Father's business to help one another finish well! *"Even when we were dead in sins, hath (God) quickened us together with Christ (by grace ye are saved); And hath raised us up together, and made us sit together in heavenly places in Christ Jesus"* (Ephesians 2: 5-6).

Whenever I'm reminded of "who wins" and helping each other win, the Holy Spirit reminds me about the "cloud of witnesses" in Hebrews 12: 1. Who are the people that are the great cloud of witnesses in our lives? Is it just the Bible heroes of the faith? I don't believe they are the only heroes. When you're sitting in church with brothers and sisters in Christ, look around you. You'll find heroes of the faith there too. As *"the Lord went before them by day in a pillar of cloud to show them the way"* (Exodus 13:21), God also uses us Christians to help show one another the way as we faithfully study and share His Word.

The Holy Spirit always wants us to remember the Prize for which we're running. Is it heaven? Is it to prosper here on earth? Is it to get the best mansion in heaven? Is it to get one of the five crowns? No, it's none of those things. The Prize is Christ – to be like Him – *"to know him, the power of His resurrection and the fellowship of his sufferings"* (Philippians 3:10). Jesus is the Prize of the high calling of God!

Running the race looking backwards doesn't work. Past accomplishments can become an anchor. We can be guided by the past – like a rudder. Better yet, I want to keep my eyes forward and my body straining toward the marked out track. *"...but this one thing I do, forgetting what is behind, and reaching forth unto those things that are before, I press toward the mark for the prize of the high calling of God in Christ Jesus"* (Philippians 3: 13-14).

WHAT DOES THE FINISH LINE LOOK LIKE TO YOU?

The "Thief" Becomes Our Judge – The Judgment Seat of Christ

So, do you see the finish line? What does it look like to you? Once again, the finish line is at the Judgment Seat of Christ. It's when we all appear together at that place. It happens after the "Rapture of the Church." Can you see the billions – like the stars in the sky – gathering before Christ?

So, brother in Christ, do you see the finish line? Do you see yourself carrying another brother that you helped overcome his alcohol addiction, or his anger, or whatever other sin was a weight that dragged him down in the race?

Sister in Christ, do you see yourself arm-in-arm with other sisters who needed your phone calls, visits, and prayers to overcome the pressures of life?

Pastors who embrace the values of the cross of Christ as a good shepherd will be surrounded by many they don't know. These strangers will thank the pastors for their great love and care. The pastor will say, "When did I show you love and care?" They will answer, "When you were a Christlike role model and faithfully preached to my relative, friend, or neighbor – because they then shared your message and themselves with me as you taught them."

You faithful teacher will cross that finish line with kids and adults you don't know along with your Sunday School or Bible study class. You overcame your own insecurity about being a teacher and trusted Jesus. You emulated Christ. You taught your people to lead others to Christ and now you see the results.

You deacon finish well with the parents, friends, and relatives of someone in your congregation because you remembered to faithfully keep them in prayer after you heard a prayer request shared at church.

You single-person finish arm-in-arm with those you faithfully fellowshipped and served with. You hear, "Well done thou good and faithful servant."

You mother and father finish with your kids. And you hug the Sunday school, Bible study teacher, or youth leader who led them to the Lord and gave them those solid Christian foundational values.

Don't be the Christian who finishes by the "skin of his teeth". He finishes rather empty-handed and regrets all the missed opportunities to "touch" and help others! There will be many tears at the Judgment Seat of Christ – let them be tears of joy – not tears shed for miserably missing ministry.

How much more time do you and I have to run this race? Only God knows. He comes, as you very well know, as a thief in the night! We must run well, help others finish well, and keep our eyes on the finish line.

VISION OF THE JUDGMENT SEAT OF CHRIST

Here's a vision that can illuminate our thinking about this judgment of us by Christ. I believe it helps us better realize how we should be preparing for His second coming.

One summer day, I was invited to address 60 pastors and leaders of a major denomination. It was exciting for me to think about what might result from giving "seed" to these "sowers" of the gospel. That afternoon, the Virginia sun was burning brightly and I decided to rest a while. As I contemplated what the Lord had given me to say, I fell into a deep sleep, and was launched into a heavenly realm where I stood with ten thousand times ten thousand and thousands of thousands.

They were from every kindred, tongue, people, and nation. In the midst of these vast numbers of people stood a Judgment Seat and there in all His glory was Christ, Himself. At first, He was so bright that I couldn't tell it was Him; but it soon became apparent that this glorious person was my Lord. All the people praised Him and the sound of their cheers was deafening.

I joined in the singing and praising, and then something very strange happened. Jesus looked at me. It seemed that the Lord's eye caught the eye of everyone at the same time. It was probably like what happened to Peter – after he had denied the Lord three times – when Jesus looked at him. The noise of the crowd seemed to hush and I could only see Christ's eye. The Lord's look must have only lasted a moment, but it seemed to me like a lifetime. I had experienced being heart-to-heart with the Lord, but now we were eye-to-eye.

I was lifted to spiritual heights unknown to me till then. I saw a stability -surpassing the tallest of earth's mountains; a strength – surpassing the combined force of the wind and ocean during a violent storm; a purity - surpassing the smallest of infants; a peace - surpassing the most tranquil waters; a deep, genuine care and concern – surpassing a mother's love for her nursing child; a joy - surpassing a father who receives back his rebellious son; and, a hope - surpassing the runner about the pass the finish line first.

With that look, it seemed that the Lord searched to see His own image in me. Though Jesus was looking in me for a reflection of Himself, I began to see myself reflected back to me. I began to see certain events from my life - they were opportunities I had missed to share the gospel or to emulate Christ – they were times when I had worked for Christ in my own strength and not in His strength. Tears flowed over my face as I viewed these things - for I saw them being burned up like wood, hay, and stubble.

Then my eyes, as if controlled by a source outside myself, viewed more and more of the Lord's face – not just His eye. When I caught a glimpse of His mouth, the Lord began to smile with such warmth that my tears were dried up instantly and I began to feel a certain glow about me. Then the Lord spoke to me. He called me by a new name, "Jom" and said, "Enter the joy of your Lord and let me show you the pyramid of your life." When I heard the Lord call me by another name, I was puzzled because the Lord had called me "Jim" in my dream so many years before. Knowing this, Jesus explained, "I called you "Jim" when you were searching to know Me. You were still living for yourself. You still had the "I" in the center of your life. But as you allowed yourself to be transformed, My name for you became "Jom", because you put Me and Others in the center instead of yourself!"

And then I was put into a pyramid with others whom I recognized and knew during my lifetime. They were all arranged into an upside down pyramid with me at the very bottom. And they were all rejoicing! The Lord then pointed to each one of these people and began to tell me what happened to them. The Lord began, "Do you remember this lady who was on the bus, who was almost ready to deny My existence? You ran after her, witnessed to her, and she received Me there in the parking lot. Do you remember? She became a Sunday school teacher and led many children to accept me also." And as He spoke, those rejoicing children – that I had never met - were added to the pyramid.

"Remember this young man in your singles' group who became a pastor? He got a church in the inner city and he was put in charge of inner city ministry in the largest city in New Jersey. He made disciples who also went on to bring My gospel to many inner city people." When He said that, more rejoicing people that I never met were added and the pyramid got even bigger. Then pointing to a group of people who were with me in the pyramid, the Lord said, "Do you remember these sixty people who accepted Me during the lay witness mission that you led? They each brought one more to me." And more rejoicing people were added to the pyramid.

The Lord continued to tell me about the young soldier, who I had helped find his way back to Christ, the lesbian, who had accepted Him and became a Sunday school teacher, all the members of my Sunday school classes, workshops, and seminars. There were many that I had touched that I was unaware of – some were children of parents I had helped stay together – others were people I had prayed for unceasingly, not knowing any of the results. All of them were there rejoicing!

As I looked at everyone in the pyramid above me, I remembered what the Apostle Paul had told the Thessalonians, *"For what is our hope, or joy, or crown of rejoicing? Are not even ye in the presence of our Lord Jesus Christ at his coming? For ye are our glory and joy"* (1 Thessalonians 2:19-20). I realized that the Lord had created a *crown of rejoicing* people all around me!

When the Lord finished speaking with me, I noticed that I was not at the very bottom of this pyramid. Esther, the woman who led me to Christ, was under me. And I was only a small part of her crown. Under her was another, and another further down, and that continued further and further downward. At the very bottom of the pyramid, with an uncountable number in His crown, was Christ. He said, "Do you remember when I told you that if you would be the greatest in My kingdom, you should be the servant of all? I told you, *'Whosoever desires to be first among you, let him be your slave – just as the Son of Man did not come to be served but to serve, and to give his life a ransom for many'"* (Matthew 20: 27-28). I realized that Jesus was First and Last – that He was the Source as well as the Finish Line of my faith. But there was something even below Christ. I realized, after a while of straining to see, that at the very bottom of the pyramid was the image of a broken heart – it was the Father's broken heart! But His heart was healed!

Suddenly, I felt another crown upon my head and the Lord said, "Behold your hope, and joy, and crown of rejoicing. Are not these people, whom you touched and to whom you ministered in your lifetime, who are now in My presence, your hope, joy, and crown?" Then without delay I cast that crown at the Lord's feet and these words fell effortlessly from my lips, *"You alone are worthy, O Lord, to receive the glory and honor and power"* (Revelation 4:11). Immediately the space around me became brilliant with light. And I remembered what Daniel had said, *"They that turn many to righteousness shall shine as the stars forever and ever"* (Daniel 12:3).

Then I heard a voice coming from the throne of God saying, *"Praise our God, all you His servants, and you who fear Him, both small and great"* (Revelation 19:5). And I heard once again the thundering of the great crowd saying, *"Alleluia, for the Lord God Omnipotent reigns! Let us be glad and rejoice and give honor to Him for the marriage supper of the Lamb is come, and His wife has made herself ready"* (Revelation 19:6-7)!

Then I and the others were led to the Marriage Feast of the Lamb where we were now said to have *"made ourselves ready"* and were *"arrayed in fine linen, clean and white,"* which represented all the righteous acts of the millions in Christ's presence. Revelation 19:8.

When I awoke, I fell to my knees and rededicated my life to Christ. I asked forgiveness for not using every opportunity the Lord had given me to share Christ with others; and also for the times I lived by flesh rather than living by faith and trust in Christ. I wanted more than ever before to tell people about Him – His stability, strength, purity, love, joy, peace, and hope – to tell Christians about their appointment with Him at the Judgment Seat. I started by telling the pastors that day and they went on to sow that seed in many other hearts. I will meet them all on that great Judgment Seat day in my crown of rejoicing!

CHAPTER 11

THE "THIEF" BECOMES OUR BRIDEGROOM – A MARRIAGE MADE IN HEAVEN

The One who told us to prepare for Him to come *"like a thief in the night"* is Himself preparing a huge banquet for us. Jesus has a grand purpose in His return. He's coming to take His bride to His Father's house to consummate the marriage and celebrate the union at an extraordinary marriage feast, called the Marriage Supper of the Lamb. It reminds me of "The *Last* Supper" except it should be called "The *Lasting* Supper." When Jesus was explaining His second coming, He spoke about men being ready to receive their master who was returning from a wedding feast. And if the servants were ready, He would put on the garments of a servant, and serve his servants.

"Be dressed ready for service and keep your lamps burning, like men waiting for their master to return from a wedding banquet, so that when he comes and knocks they can immediately open the door for him. It will be good for those servants whose master finds them watching when he comes. I tell you the truth, he will dress himself to serve, will have them recline at the table and will come and wait on them" (Luke 12:35-37).

THE CHURCH IS THE BRIDE OF CHRIST

The New Testament describes the Church of Jesus Christ in several ways. There are seven symbols that represent the Church:

He is the Good Shepherd and we are the sheep. John 10:1-18.

We are "living stones" in a building and Jesus is the Cornerstone. 1Peter 2:4-7.

Jesus is the True Vine and Christians are the branches. John 15:1

We are merchants who buy a single pearl of great price. Jesus is the Pearl. Matthew 13:45.

Jesus is the Great High Priest over the household of faith and we are His servant-priests. Hebrews 4:14-16.

The Church is the Body of Christ. We are members of one another, and we are all under the direction of the Head, Jesus Christ. 1 Corinthians 12:12-14.

Finally, the Church is the BRIDE OF CHRIST and Jesus is the WAITING BRIDEGROOM. The Apostle Paul, when speaking to the Corinthian church, said, *"I am jealous for you with a godly jealousy. I promised you to one husband, to Christ, so that I might present you as a pure virgin to him"* (2Corinthians 11:2).

On another occasion, Paul spoke to the Ephesians about husbands loving their wives like Christ loved the Church, His bride. *"Husbands love your wives, just as Christ loved the church and gave himself up for her to make her holy, cleansing her by the washing with water through the word, and to present her to himself as a radiant church, without stain or wrinkle or any other blemish, but holy and blameless...This is a profound mystery – but I am talking about Christ and the church"* (Ephesians 5:25-32).

The "Thief" Becomes Our Bridegroom – A Marriage Made In Heaven

In Revelation 21:9, *"One of the seven angels who had the seven bowls full of the seven last plaques came and said to me [the Apostle John], 'Come, I will show you the bride, the wife of the Lamb [Christ].'"* The bride here was the New Jerusalem filled with all the believers of Christ.

THE TRADITIONAL ORIENTAL MARRIAGE

The traditional oriental marriage has three major steps:

The legal marriage is consummated by the parents when a dowry is paid. For Christians that happens when we receive (trust) Jesus as Savior. The dowry has been paid by Christ's sacrifice on the cross. So the bride has been purchased by the Bridegroom in the legal sense

After the legal marriage – and after the bridegroom prepares a place for his bride in his father's house – the bridegroom goes with his friends to the bride's house to take her back to his home. For Christians this will happen at the Rapture of the Church. 1Thessalonians 4:17. Jesus said He would return so *"that where I am, there ye may be also"* (John 14: 1-3).

The bridal procession would be followed by the marriage feast, which would often last for many days. John 2. This event is fulfilled in heaven (Revelation 19:7-9) just before the time of Christ's return to earth to establish His earthly kingdom. In this scripture, the Church is already seen as the wife of the Lamb and as already arrayed in fine linen.

The marriage consists of all the events after the coming of the Bridegroom for the bride. In this ceremony is the marriage supper, which is the meal. An invitation is extended to those not part of the Church to participate in the marriage supper. Revelation 19:9. These guests might include the Old Testament saints and those martyrs from the Tribulation period (Revelation 20:4-6) who are raised at Christ's Second Coming [His return to earth] as well as those who are alive at the beginning of the millennium reign of Christ. The entire human race was invited – but only a fraction will attend. The gospel of Jesus Christ is the invitation! It's gone out throughout the centuries from Old Testament times to the present day. Some accept it. Some reject it.

AN OLD TESTAMENT PICTURE OF GETTING A WIFE

Genesis 24 gives us an early picture of the way God the Father would later send the Holy Spirit into the world to call out a bride for His Son.

ABRAHAM represents the FATHER. Jesus described it like *"a certain king who would make a marriage for his son"* (Matthew 22:2; John 6:44).

Abraham made a covenant with his **SERVANT** to return to his homeland to find a wife for his son Isaac. This servant represents the HOLY SPIRIT. The servant doesn't speak of Himself but takes the things of the Bridegroom to win the bride. John 16: 13-14. He enriches the bride with the Bridegroom's gifts. Galatians 5:22; 1Corinthians 12:7-11. He also brings the bride to the Bridegroom. Acts 13:4; Romans 8:11; 1Thessalonians 4:14-16.

REBEKAH represents a type of the CHURCH (the Greek word is "ekklesia"), the called out bride of Christ. 2Corinthians 11:2; Ephesians 5:25-32.

ISAAC is a type of the BRIDEGROOM, *"whom not having seen the bride"* loves her through the testimony of the servant. 1Peter 1:8. The bridegroom goes out to meet and receive the bride. 1Thessalonians 4: 16-18.

CHAPTER 12

THE "THIEF" BECOMES OUR COMMANDER-IN-CHIEF- THE BATTLE OF ARMAGEDDON

MORE THAN CONQUERORS IN CHRIST

The One who told us to prepare for Him to come *"like a thief in the night"* is Himself preparing to lead us in battle. The second coming of Christ is in two phases. The first is the Rapture of the Church, which we've spoken about previously. That first phase is when Jesus comes as a *"thief in the night"* because no one knows when that will be. The second phase is when Christ returns at the Battle of Armageddon. We know that it happens seven years after the Rapture and just after the Marriage Supper of the Lamb. Revelation 19:5-21.

At the Rapture, we receive immortal bodies. At the Judgment Seat of Christ we receive light, like the brightness of the stars (Daniel 3:12). And at the marriage supper, all believers, as the bride of Christ, receive garments of fine linen, clean and white. Revelation 19:8. All aglow like stars, wearing these garments, we now become part of the *"armies of heaven,"* (vs.14) and we follow Christ (the Sun of Righteousness) to meet armies of all unbelieving nations, the Antichrist and the False Prophet at a place called in Hebrew *Armageddon.* Revelation 16:16.

The promise given to Abraham by the Lord – that his descendents would be as numerous as the *stars* in heaven - is literally fulfilled. The Sun of Righteousness will be followed by a mantle of tiny stars (i.e. believers) flowing and glowing behind Him. *He [the Lord] took him [Abraham] outside and said, 'Look up at the heavens and count the stars – if indeed you count them.' Then he said to him, 'So shall your offspring be'"* (Genesis 15:4-5).

On earth, we have been *"more than conquerors through Christ"* (Romans 8:37) wearing *"the whole armor of God"* (Ephesians 6:13). At this second coming of Christ, we are privileged to become warriors and ride with Christ into the final battle, who by the *"sword that proceeds out of His mouth"* (Revelation 19:15) wins the battle against all evil. Revelation 11:15 is fulfilled, *"The kingdoms of this world have become the kingdoms of our God and His Christ; and he shall reign forever and ever."*

HOW THE BATTLE UNFOLDS

Satan and his demons have deceived world leaders. *"They are spirits of demons performing miraculous signs, and they go out to the kings of the whole world, to gather them for the battle on* **the great day of God Almighty**. *'Behold I come like a thief! Blessed is he who stays awake and keeps his clothes with him, so he may not go naked and be shamefully exposed.' Then they gathered the kings together to one place that in Hebrew is called Armageddon"* (Revelation 16: 14-16).

The prophet Zechariah put it this way, *"I will gather all the nations to Jerusalem to fight against it; the city will be captured, the houses ransacked, and the women raped. Half the city will go into exile, but the rest of the people will not be taken from the city. Then the Lord will go out and fight against those nations, as he fights in the day of battle. On that day his feet will stand on the Mount of Olives, east of Jerusalem, and the Mount of Olives will be split in two from east to west, forming a great valley, with half of the mountain moving north and half moving south"* (Zechariah 14:2–4). Also note vs. 5, *"...and the Lord my God shall come, and all the saints with thee."* (The statement *"the mount of Olives will be split"* is due to the earthquake referred to in Revelation 16:18-19)

In Revelation 17: 12-15, the angel reveals to John how the kings of the earth delegate their power to a one-world government leader called "the beast" [the Antichrist]. *"For God has put it in their hearts to execute His purpose by having a common purpose, and by giving their kingdom to the beast, until the words of God will be fulfilled"* (Revelation 17:17).

THE BATTLE DETAILS

Revelation 19:11-13 says, " *And I saw heaven opened, and behold, a white horse, and He who sat on it is called Faithful and True, and in righteousness He judges and wages war. His eyes are a flame of fire, and on His head are many diadems[crowns]; and He has a name written on Him which no one knows except Himself. He is clothed with a robe dipped in blood, and His name is called The Word of God."* Also see Isaiah 63:1-4, 6.

"See, the Lord is coming with fire, and his chariots are like a whirlwind; he will bring down his anger with fury, and his rebuke with flames of fire. For with fire and with his sword the Lord will execute judgment upon all men, and many will be those slain by the Lord" (Isaiah 66:15-16). Christ is depicted with clothes stained red with blood because He shed His precious blood for humanity and is now going into battle against those who rejected His sacrifice. Also, because He now destroys all those who oppose Him. It is the final battle for RIGHTEOUSNESS in which He overcomes the forces of evil in order for the Kingdom of God to be established on this earth. The "beast" and all his human followers are defeated in this Battle of Armageddon.

Revelation 19:15-16 says, *"From His mouth comes a sharp sword, so that with it He may strike down the nations, and He will rule them with a rod of iron; and He treads the wine press of the fierce wrath of God, the Almighty. And on His robe and on His thigh He has a name written, 'KING OF KINGS, AND LORD OF LORDS.' Then I saw an angel standing in the sun, and he cried out with a loud voice, saying to all the birds which fly in mid-heaven, 'Come, assemble for the great supper of God' (vs18) so that you may eat the flesh of kings and the flesh of commanders and the flesh of mighty men and the flesh of horses and of those who sit on them and the flesh of all men, both free men and slaves, and small and great."*

"This is the plague with which the Lord will strike all the nations that fought against Jerusalem: Their flesh will rot while they are still standing on their feet, their eyes will rot in their sockets and their tongues will rot in their mouths" (Zechariah 14: 12).

Finally, the beast and the false prophet are taken, and cast into the lake of fire. Revelation 19:19-20 says, *"And I saw the beast and the kings of the earth and their armies assembled to make war against Him who sat on the horse and against His army. And the beast was seized, and with him the false prophet who performed the signs in his presence, by which he deceived those who had received the mark of the beast and those who worshiped his image; these two were thrown alive into the lake of fire which burns with brimstone."*

CHAPTER 13

THE "THIEF" BECOMES OUR KING - RULING & REIGNING WITH CHRIST

The One who told us to prepare for Him to come *"like a thief in the night"* is Himself preparing to rule on earth as King with us ruling and reigning with Him. This will be a glorious kingdom. The Bible speaks many times about the reign of Christ and those who will rule with Him. 1Corinthians 6:1-3 says that the Church will judge the world and angels. Revelation 5:10 says, *"He [the Lamb of God] has made us kings and priests to our God: And we shall reign on the earth."* When speaking of our eternal home, Revelation 22:5 says, *"There shall be no night there: They need no lamp nor light of the sun, for the Lord God gives them [His servants] light. And they shall reign forever and ever."*

I'm not sure what our individual duties will be but we will have a place in the Lord's kingdom, some greater than others. This is apparent in many scriptures throughout the Bible, but never clearer than in Luke 19:12-27. In this passage, Jesus was sharing a parable with the multitude about the importance of faithfulness to God and how it would reflect on their stature in His future kingdom. In the parable, He explains that there were three different servants who were given equal amounts of money by their master. They were instructed to go out and invest or do business with the money. After a certain amount of time had passed, the master came and asked the three servants to give an account. The first servant presented his earnings, and had done well. He gained ten times what the master gave him. The second servant also presented his earnings, and he managed to increase his money five times. The last servant did nothing with his money and was found to be unfaithful. The first two servants, because of their faithfulness, were given ten and five cities, respectively, to rule over. The last servant, who did nothing with his money was reprimanded and his money taken from him. So shall it be in that great and marvelous day when Jesus comes to rule and reign. Those who have been faithful with the talents and gifts God has given them will be rewarded accordingly.

In that day, I believe many Christians will make it to heaven by the skin of their teeth, having spent much of their lives placing themselves first instead the Lord and others. They will suffer loss and make it in *"so as by fire"* (1Corinthians 3:13-15).

If you think for one moment that heaven is a place of equal opportunity you have another think coming. Even though you may feel that you just want to make it in, and that's all that matters, your thinking will change dramatically the minute you see Jesus. For in a moment, you will learn what your full potential as a Christian could have been and the reality of what it truly was. Many will be shocked to tears when they realize the lives that could have been changed and the impact they could have made on those around them if they had only obeyed. This will be a tragic time for those Christians.

But for those who were faithful to prepare themselves for Christ's return as we have described, they will be exalted before the Lord and rewarded with cities to reign over during the 1000-year reign and beyond. Of course, they may not reach their full potential either, but they will be rewarded for what they did do with the talents God gave them.

Yes, faithfulness and obedience will be key indicators as to how high we will rank throughout eternity. For it is the Lord's will that we all achieve the standard set before us with the talents He has granted us. May you and I be found faithful in that glorious day of our Lord and Savior Jesus Christ.

TRIBULATION SAINTS WILL ALSO RULE

"And I saw thrones, and they sat upon them, and judgment [or authority to rule] was given unto them: And I saw the souls of them that were beheaded for the witness of Jesus, and for the word of God, and which had not worshipped the beast, neither his image, neither had received his mark upon their foreheads, or in their hands; and they lived and reigned with Christ a thousand years" (Revelation 20:4).

This passage of scripture identifies a multitude of people who have resurrected bodies just like our Lord Jesus Christ. These people were alive at the Rapture when Christ took His bride away. They are identified in Revelation 7:9-17 as those who were left behind but refused to take the mark of the beast and were slain for their witness of Christ. These are the martyred saints who were killed during the tribulation period and their number is said to be so great that no man could number them.

When Christ comes in the clouds of glory to rule and reign on earth they will be resurrected. As mentioned above, they are promised a place in the millennial reign of Christ. Some hold to the view that they will act as servants in the millennium temple due to their description in Revelation 7:15 which states, *"Therefore are they before the throne of God, and serve him day and night in his temple: And he that sitteth on the throne shall dwell among them."*

Whatever their position, it is certain that they will have a special place in His kingdom, for He will dwell among them.

WHY MUST THE LORD RULE WITH A ROD OF IRON?

Revelation 2:27 and 19:15 tell us that the Lord will rule with a rod of iron. As unbelievable as it seems, however, there will still be those who will oppose Him. They will find out quickly that all offenders are swiftly punished.

Everyone will make the trip to the holy city once a year and take part in worshipping the Lord. Those who refuse will not receive rain for their crops (Zechariah 14: 17, 18), and God will curse the ground that they plant. Many will give the Lord lip service for the sake of prosperity, but in their heart, they will be far from Him.

You may ask, "With all the prosperity and peaceful surroundings (see the scriptural references given below), why would anyone rebel against God? Besides, Satan is bound for a thousand years and won't be able to tempt man to sin!" It's true that this world will be free of the tempting power of Satan for one thousand years. Why then would the Lord have to rule the world with a rod of iron? After all, isn't Satan the reason why we sin? Not at all! Every person that is born into this world is born with a sin nature. Psalm 51:5. Even though everyone who is granted to enter into the millennium will be saved and filled with the Spirit, as time goes on, that will change.

During this millennium, there will be a population explosion, and as each generation passes, men will begin to resist the grace of the Lord and choose their own way. They will not want to retain the Lord in their hearts. This rebellion will not be an outward uprising, for the Lord will not allow that, but a rebellion of the heart. Though they will obey, it will only be for the purpose of receiving blessings from the Lord.

You may still question, "How could this be possible?" The answer is that Satan is not the reason we rebel against God. Rebellion is born within every man and resides within the sin nature. Satan only uses this nature to manipulate us to sin against God. Even though Satan has been bound for one thousand years, and even though the Lord will greatly bless man both physically and spiritually, some will still choose to follow their sin nature as opposed to allowing the Spirit nature to rule their lives. Through all the prosperity, peace and even the absence of Satan, many men and women will still choose in their hearts to live in rebellion against God. This confirms that man is a sinner in need of a Savior.

So, at the end of the thousand-year reign of Christ, when Satan is released on the earth again, he will find many eager to follow him. Revelation 20:7-10. But God will waste no time destroying them. (vs. 9).

WHAT THE WORLD IS LIKE DURING THE 1000-YEAR REIGN

Jeremiah 23:5 – Christ shall be King. *"'The days are coming,' declares the LORD, 'when I will raise up to David a righteous Branch, a King who will reign wisely and do what is just and right in the land.'"*

Isaiah 2: 1-3 - Israel will be prominent. *"This is what Isaiah son of Amoz saw concerning Judah and Jerusalem: In the last days the mountain of the Lord's temple will be established as chief among the mountains; it will be raised above the hills, and all nations will stream to it. Many peoples will come and say, 'Come, let us go up to the mountain of the LORD, to the house of the God of Jacob. He will teach us his ways, so that we may walk in his paths.' The law will go out from Zion, the word of the LORD from Jerusalem."*

His rule will reflect His character:

Isaiah 2: 4 – Justice. *"He will judge between the nations and will settle disputes for many peoples. They will beat their swords into plowshares and their spears into pruning hooks. Nation will not* *take up sword against nation, nor will they train for war anymore."*

Micah 4: 1-4 – All prosper. *"In the last days the mountain of the Lord's temple will be established as chief among the mountains; it will be raised above the hills, and peoples will stream to it. Many nations will come and say, 'Come, let us go up to the mountain of the LORD, to the house of the God of Jacob. He will teach us his ways, so that we may walk in his paths.' The law will go out from Zion, the word of the LORD from Jerusalem. He will judge between many peoples and will settle disputes for strong nations far and wide. They will beat their swords into plowshares and their spears into pruning hooks. Nation will not take up sword against nation, nor will they train for war anymore. Every man will sit under his own vine and under his own fig tree, and no one will make them afraid, for the LORD Almighty has spoken."*

Jeremiah 23: 5 – Righteousness. *"'The days are coming,' declares the LORD, 'when I will raise up to David a righteous Branch, a King who will reign wisely and do what is just and right in the land.'"*

Zechariah 8: 4-5 – Peace. *"This is what the LORD Almighty says: 'Once again men and women of ripe old age will sit in the streets of Jerusalem, each with cane in hand because of his age. The city streets will be filled with boys and girls playing there.'"*

Jeremiah 23: 4 – People safe. *"'I will place shepherds over them who will tend them, and they will no longer be afraid or terrified, nor will any be missing,' declares the LORD.'"*

The natural world is transformed...

Isaiah 30: 23-26 - Climate. *"He will also send you rain for the seed you sow in the ground, and the food that comes from the land will be rich and plentiful. In that day your cattle will graze in* broad meadows. *The oxen and donkeys that work the soil will eat fodder and mash, spread out with fork and shovel. In the day of great slaughter, when the towers fall, streams of water will flow on every high mountain and every lofty hill. The moon will shine like the sun, and the sunlight will be seven times brighter, like the light of seven full days, when the LORD binds up the bruises of his people and heals the wounds he inflicted."*

Isaiah 11: 6-8 – Animals tame. *"The wolf will live with the lamb, the leopard will lie down with the goat, the calf and the lion and the yearling together; and a little child will lead them. The cow will feed with the bear, their young will lie down together, and the lion will eat straw like the ox. The infant will play near the hole of the cobra, and the young child put his hand into the viper's nest."*

Ezekiel 47: 9-10 – Great fishing. *"Swarms of living creatures will live wherever the river flows. There will be large numbers of fish, because this water flows there and makes the salt water fresh; so where the river flows everything will live. Fishermen will stand along the shore; from En Gedi to En Eglaim there will be places for spreading nets. The fish will be of many kinds--like the fish of the Great Sea."*

Isaiah 65: 19-20, 22 – Life is lengthened. *"I will rejoice over Jerusalem and take delight in my people; the sound of weeping and of crying will be heard in it no more. "Never again will there be in it an infant who lives but a few days, or an old man who does not live out his years; he who dies at a hundred will be thought a mere youth; he who fails to reach a hundred will be considered accursed. No longer will they build houses and others live in them, or plant and others eat. For as the days of a tree, so will be the days of my people; my chosen ones will long enjoy the works of their hands."*

Ezekiel 47: 12 – Trees provide food and medicine. *"Fruit trees of all kinds will grow on both banks of the river. Their leaves will not wither, nor will their fruit fail. Every month they will bear,* *because the water from the sanctuary flows to them. Their fruit will serve for food and their leaves for healing."*

Malachi 1: 11- God will be worshipped and Christ's name known in all the world. *"My name will be great among the nations, from the rising to the setting of the sun. In every place incense and pure offerings will be brought to my name, because my name will be great among the nations," says the LORD Almighty."*

Zechariah 14: 16 - Representatives come to see Him in Jerusalem. *"Then the survivors from all the nations that have attacked Jerusalem will go up year after year to worship the King, the LORD Almighty, and to celebrate the Feast of Tabernacles."*

CHAPTER 14

THE "THIEF" BECOMES OUR ETERNAL RESIDENCE BUILDER - THE NEW JERUSALEM

The One who told us to prepare for Him to come *"like a thief in the night"* is Himself preparing a home for us believers in heaven. Our eyes have never seen such beauty. Our ears have never heard the sounds of it. And our minds have never imagined it. *"No eye has seen, no ear heard, no mind conceived what God has prepared for those who love him"* (1Corinthians 2:9). *"...for he [God] has prepared a city for them"* (Hebrews 11:16). It's a place that will satisfy every desire of our hearts as well as being a majestic home that glorifies the King of kings and the Lord of lords, our Lord Jesus Christ. It's called The New Jerusalem, and *"the Lord God Almighty and the Lamb are the temple of it"* (Revelation 21:22).

HEAVEN

Moses got a glimpse of the real Heaven because God gave him a pattern on the mountain to build the tabernacle after the one he had seen in heaven. It has so many symbols of Christ's life:

The altars represent His sacrifice for us – The Lamb of God. John 1:29, 36.

The mercy seat represents Christ, the propitiation for our sins that brings God's mercy. Romans 3:25.

The showbread represents Christ, the Bread of Life. John 6:35.

The candlestick represents Christ, the Light of the World. John 8:12.

The laver represents Christ, the one who cleanses our sins – though they are red as scarlet, He washes us white as snow. Isaiah 1:18.

John saw an altar (part of the tabernacle in heaven). Under it, he saw the souls of those who were beheaded for their testimony of Jesus Christ during the Great Tribulation period. Revelation 6: 9-10.

HEAVEN'S THRONE ROOM

In Revelation 4:1- 11, John saw what we might call a throne room in heaven (v2). The One who sat on the throne looked like a gem stone – bright and sparkling with light (v2) like Jasper and a Sardine stone. Jasper is found in all colors including: red, brown, pink, yellow, green, grey/white, and shades of blue and purple. It comes in a variety of patterns that look like landscapes of mountains and valleys. It was found in the High Priest's breastplate, representing one of the 12 tribes of Israel. Exodus 39:8-14. Sardine Stone is a gem of blood red color. It's also found in the High Priest's breastplate. Remember, God is Spirit!

There is a rainbow around the throne that looked to John like an emerald – green and sparkling. Revelation 4:3. He also saw 24 seats around the throne, with 24 elders seated there with crowns of gold on their heads. (v4). They continually praised the Lord saying, *"Thou are worthy, O Lord, to receive glory and honor and power: for thou hast created all things, and for thy glory they are and were created"* (v11). He also heard thunder and lightning and voices coming out of the throne. There were also seven burning lamps before the throne, which are the seven Spirits of God (vs. 5-6).

Before the throne was a sea of glass like crystal (v6) and in the midst of the throne and around the throne were Living Creatures, who never rested night and day saying, *"Holy, Holy, Lord God Almighty, which was, and is, and is to come"* (v8). They had four faces that represent the life of Christ:

The face of a Lion represents Jesus the Lion of the tribe of Judah.

The face of a Calf represents Jesus the sacrificial Lamb of God.

The face of a Man represents Jesus, God incarnate.

The face of a Flying Eagle represents Jesus the returning King of kings.

THE HEAVENLY CITY WHOSE BUILDER AND MAKER IS GOD - THE NEW JERUSALEM

God creates a new heaven and new earth. Revelation 21:1. Then John sees a city, whose builder and maker is God (Hebrews 11:10), coming down out of the new heaven. Revelation 21:2 – 22:5.

Have you ever gotten your house ready for family and friends to see for the first time? Have you ever done that when you've been out of State or out of the country? What's the first thing you do when they arrive? Answer: You show them around your house!

I think that's the way Jesus felt in John 14: 1-3 when He was anticipating His return to bring His people back to His Father's house. And, it's probably the way He feels when one of us go to be with Him in death. He wants to show us around His city that

He's prepared for those who love Him. It's His City. He's the Designer. Hebrews 11:10. And He built it for us! Hebrews 11:16.

I have two names for this city that mean a lot to me. The first is "Honeymoon City." It's where Jesus is preparing a place for us to spend eternity with Him (John 14:1-3). It's "out of sight" right now (like honeymooners who go to be alone after the wedding). But the city will not always remain "out of sight." Revelation 20:6; 21:1. We'll dwell there together with the Lord, and we'll see His face; and His name will be in our foreheads. The city is ever bright with Christ, the Light of the World. Revelation 21:23. There's never night there! Revelation 22: 3-5. When John saw it for the first time, he said the city was like a bride adorned for her husband. Revelation 21:2.

My other favorite name for The New Jerusalem is "Showcase City." Have you ever revisited your old High School or College, and been drawn to the showcases of trophies and awards that your school won during the years you attended? Well, "Showcase City" is the Lord's display case for the results of His redeeming work on behalf of humanity. *"And the building of the wall of it [the city] was of jasper: and the city was pure gold **like clear glass"*** (Revelation 21:18).

What's on display in this showcase? Answer: All believers in the Lord Jesus Christ sparkle like precious jewels (or stars – Daniel 12:3) in "Showcase City." We are its inhabitants and we are the Lord's awards and trophies. We'll look like the precious stones that form the foundation of the city (Revelation 21:19-21). Stones shaped in the "heat" of the race of life! It's like the final victory lap for Christians. The crowds that once shouted for us to glorify self and follow the world, flesh, and the devil will be gone forever! People on earth, who *"shall walk in the light of it* [the city]*"* (Revelation 21:24), are eternally reminded of God's great victory through Christ!

The "Thief" Becomes Our Eternal Residence Builder – The New Jerusalem

WHAT'S THE CITY LIKE? HOW IS IT ADORNED?

The New Jerusalem – the home Jesus has designed and built for us – has twelve gates with the names of the twelve tribes of Israel inscribed there. Revelation 21:12. Each gate is made of one pearl. Revelation 21:21; Matthew 13:25-26. The Lord God Almighty and the Lamb are its temple. Revelation 21:22.

It has twelve foundations, being the most important parts of any construction because they support everything else. These foundations have the names of the apostles inscribed on them. Revelation 21:14. Remember Jude 3, *"...and exhort you to earnestly contend for the faith which was once delivered unto the saints."* That means the faith that Christ and the apostles delivered to us!

The foundations are made up of 12 layers of precious gems – like the gems we are becoming as we grow more and more from within like Jesus (1 Corinthians 3:10-17) to build God's temple (v17). These gems represent the work of the saints that is tested, tried, and true - work (i.e. fruit) for the kingdom that is not in our own strength but in Christ's strength. These precious jewels are exactly the same as all twelve gems in the High Priest's breastplate.

Streets are pure gold like transparent glass. Revelation 21:21; 1Peter1:7. The City itself is 1400 miles wide, long, and high with the river of life flowing *"from the throne of God and the Lamb."* On both sides of the river grows the tree of life, which will bear 12 different fruits – one for every month. Revelation 21:16; 22:1-2.

The throne of God and the Lamb shall be in it (Revelation 22:3) and there's no need for any external light source because the Lord God gives us light. (22:4-5).

WHO'S THERE TO SEE THIS GREAT DISPLAY?

As mentioned earlier, the nations of those who are saved – after the devil leads his rebellion against Christ – shall walk in the light of the New Jerusalem. Revelation 21:24-26. They are the ones we shall *"rule and reign forever and ever"* (Revelation 22:5). After this rebellion, the White Throne Judgment comes, where all unbelievers from all time will be cast into the lake of fire with Satan and his demons. Revelation 21:15.

With a new heaven, new earth, and New Jerusalem, God's house is with man and He will live there. No more crying, sorrow, pain, or death. The former things have passed away – there's a new dispensation, and life continues as God originally intended before the Fall. Revelation 21:1-4.

Those who believe in Jesus, receive Him as Lord and Savior, and prepare for His second coming will see and experience Jesus Christ as Judge at the Judgment Seat of Christ; as the Bridegroom at the Marriage Supper of the Lamb (The Lasting Supper); as the Commander-in-Chief of heaven's army winning the last battle for righteousness; as the King of kings and Lord of lords, ruling and reigning with Christ forever and ever; and, as the Designer, Builder, Light, Temple, and Almighty God living together with man.

"But understand this: If the owner of the house had known at what hour the thief was coming, he would not let his house be broken into. You also must be ready, because the Son of Man will come at an hour when you do not expect him." – Jesus Christ

TOPICAL INDEX

Anger – 41-42
Armor of God – 55-59, 81, 94
Battle of Armageddon – 93-96
Bitterness - 39
Born Again – 61-65, 80
Church – 89-91
Clutter of Life – 31
Course markers - 22
Crowns – 78
Discipline – 21-23
Disease – 8
Earthquake – 8
End time signs – 7-12
Envy – 40
Faith – 58, 67
Faithfulness – 16, 99
Fallen angels - 10
Fellowship – 21-22, 24-25
Finish line – 78, 82-84
Forgiveness – 67
Foundation – 36-37
Global government – 9, 10, 95
Good works – 45-49
Gospel – 7
Gossip – 42-43
Grace - 67
Heaven – 73-75, 105-110
Holy Spirit – 80-82
Honeymoon City - 108
Housekeeping of the heart – 32-35
Humility – 49
Ingratitude – 53-54

Israel – 10-11
Judgment Seat of Christ – 77-88, 93
Lake of fire – 96
Leadership – 16-17
Lordship of Christ – 35-37
Love – 44, 46
Marriage Feast – 89-93
Mercy – 49
Obedience – 44
One another – 24, 47-48
Prayer – 14-15, 21- 22, 27-28
Preparation – 16-18
Pride – 40
Rapture – 69-71, 93
Resurrection – 65
Rewards – 78-79, 84-88
Righteousness – 48-49, 58, 79, 93, 95
Ruling and reigning with Christ – 97-101
Salvation – 58, 61-65, 72-73
Science – 8
Service – 21-22, 26-27
Showcase City – 108
Slander - 41
Spiritual vitamins – 22
Spiritual warfare – 55-59
Technology – 11
Thankfulness – 51-55
The New Jerusalem – 105-110
Thousand year reign – 101-104
Transformation – 23
Unforgiveness – 39
Waiting – 18-20
Warfare – 8
Watch and wait – 13-20
Word Study – 21-22, 28-29
Worship – 21-22, 23-24

Other Books by Jim Biscardi, Jr.

Books are available on **amazon.com** and **barnesandnoble.com**. They can be ordered by any bookstore from **Ingram Books** or **Baker & Taylor**. Also contact Mantle Ministries, PO Box 248, Lanoka Harbor, NJ 08734, Tele: 609-242-8772 or Email: mantle1@att.net

www.ingramcontent.com/pod-product-compliance
Lightning Source LLC
Chambersburg PA
CBHW071301040426
42444CB00009B/1819